Internet of Things with Arduino Cookbook

Over 60 recipes will help you build smart IoT solutions and surprise yourself with captivating IoT projects you thought only existed in Bond movies

Marco Schwartz

BIRMINGHAM - MUMBAI

Internet of Things with Arduino Cookbook

First published: September 2016

Production reference: 1280916

Published by Packt Publishing Ltd.
Livery Place
35 Livery Street
Birmingham B3 2PB, UK.

ISBN 978-1-78528-658-2

www.packtpub.com

Credits

Author
Marco Schwartz

Reviewer
Vasilis Tzivaras

Commissioning Editor
Kartikey Pandey

Acquisition Editor
Prachi Bisht

Content Development Editor
Trusha Shriyan

Technical Editor
Naveenkumar Jain

Copy Editor
Safis Editing

Project Coordinator
Kinjal Bari

Proofreader
Safis Editing

Indexer
Pratik Shirodkar

Graphics
Kirk D'Penha

Production Coordinator
Shantanu N Zagade

Cover Work
Shantanu N Zagade

About the Author

Marco Schwartz is an electrical engineer, entrepreneur, and blogger. He has a master's degree in electrical engineering and computer science from Supélec, France, and a master's degree in micro engineering from the Ecole Polytechnique Fédérale de Lausanne (EPFL), Switzerland.

He has more than five years of experience working in the domain of electrical engineering. Marco's interests gravitate around electronics, home automation, the Arduino and Raspberry Pi platforms, open source hardware projects, and 3D printing.

He has several websites about Arduino, including the Open Home Automation website, which is dedicated to building home automation systems using open source hardware.

Marco has written another book on home automation and Arduino, called *Home Automation With Arduino: Automate Your Home Using Open-source Hardware*. He has also written a book on how to build Internet of Things projects with Arduino, called *Internet of Things with the Arduino Yun*, by Packt Publishing.

About the Reviewer

Vasilis Tzivaras is a software developer and hardware engineer who lives in Ioannina, Greece. He is currently an undergraduate student in the department of computer science and engineering at Ioannina. Along with his studies, he is working on many projects relevant to robotics, such as drones, home automation, and smart home systems using Arduino and the Raspberry Pi. He is also enthusiastic about clean energy solutions and cultural innovation ideas.

He has worked for the University Hospital of Ioannina as an assistant on various computer issues and has been a part of the support team of his CSE department for over a year. He has participated in IEEE UOI Student Branch and other big organizations, such as FOSSCOMM, with personal presentations for website design, programming, Linux systems, and drones.

He is the chair of IEEE University of Ioannina Student Branch and has proposed many projects and solutions to automate homes and many other life problems by reducing the time of everyday routines. In addition to this, he has come up with ideas to entertain kids with funny and magical projects using Arduino-like hardware and open source software. Many of the projects can be found on his GitHub account under the name of BillyTziv.

Apart from *Building Smart Homes with Raspberry Pi Zero* and *Internet of Things with Arduino Cookbook*, he has also published a book named *Building a Quadcopter with Arduino, by Packt Publishing*. He has also worked on another book, *Programming in C*, which is not yet published. In addition to this, he has written for blogs, forums, guides, and small chapters of books, explaining and sharing his knowledge of computers, networks, and programming.

www.PacktPub.com

eBooks, discount offers, and more

Did you know that Packt offers eBook versions of every book published, with PDF and ePub files available? You can upgrade to the eBook version at `www.PacktPub.com` and as a print book customer, you are entitled to a discount on the eBook copy. Get in touch with us at `customercare@packtpub.com` for more details.

At `www.PacktPub.com`, you can also read a collection of free technical articles, sign up for a range of free newsletters and receive exclusive discounts and offers on Packt books and eBooks.

`https://www.packtpub.com/mapt`

Get the most in-demand software skills with Mapt. Mapt gives you full access to all Packt books and video courses, as well as industry-leading tools to help you plan your personal development and advance your career.

Why Subscribe?

- Fully searchable across every book published by Packt
- Copy and paste, print, and bookmark content
- On demand and accessible via a web browser

Table of Contents

Preface

Arduino is a small single-chip computer board that can be used for a wide variety of creative hardware projects. The hardware consists of a simple microcontroller board, and chipset. It comes with a Java-based IDE that allows creators to program the board. Arduino is the ideal open hardware platform for experimenting with the world of the Internet of Things. This credit card sized Arduino board can be used via the Internet to make useful and interactive Internet of things projects.

Internet of Things, known as IoT, is changing the way we live and represents one of the biggest challenges in the IT industry. Developers are creating low cost devices that collect huge amounts of data, interact with each other, and take advantage of cloud services and cloud-based storage. Makers all over the world are working on fascinating projects that transform everyday objects into smart devices with sensors and actuators.

This book takes a recipe-based approach, giving you precise examples on how to build IoT projects using the Arduino platform.By the end of this book, you will not only know how to build these projects, but also have the skills necessary to build your own IoT projects in the future.

What this book covers

Chapter 1, Connecting an Arduino to the Web, focuses on getting you started by connecting an Arduino board to the Web. It will lay foundation for the rest of the book.

Chapter 2, Cloud Data Monitoring, deals with one of the most important thing you can do with an Internet of Things project, that is, send data online so that it can be stored, retrieved later, and plotted inside a nice dashboard.

Chapter 3, Interacting with Web Services, tells us how to use existing web services to build amazing Internet of Things projects with our Arduino board.

Chapter 4, Machine-to-Machine Interactions, focuses on something different: making two (or more) Arduino boards talk to each other and interact with each other, without any human intervention. This is known as machine-to-machine communications, which is a very exciting field of the IoT. Let's dive in!

Chapter 5, Home Automation Projects, tells us how to apply what we learned so far in this book to the home automation field. We are going to use the Arduino board to build several home automation projects that will be accessible from anywhere in the world & able to communicate with cloud services.

Chapter 6, Fun Internet of Things Projects, deals with how to build a clock that gets the time from the cloud, but also an actual GPS tracker that will display the position of your Arduino project on Google Maps!

Chapter 7, Mobile Robot Applications, tells us how to create our own mobile robot based on Arduino. Finally, to end this book about the Internet of Things, we are going to learn how to control this robot from anywhere in the world.

What you need for this book

All the projects of this chapter and this book are using Arduino MKR1000 board. This is an Arduino board released in 2016 that has an on-board WiFi connection. You can make all the projects of the book with other Arduino boards, but you might have to change part of the code

Who this book is for

This book is primarily for tech enthusiasts and early IoT adopters who would like to make the most of IoT and address the challenges encountered while developing IoT-based applications with Arduino. This book is also good for developers with basic electronics knowledge who need help to build successful Arduino projects.

Sections

In this book, you will find several headings that appear frequently (Getting ready, How to do it, How it works, There's more, and See also).

To give clear instructions on how to complete a recipe, we use these sections as follows:

Getting ready

This section tells you what to expect in the recipe, and describes how to set up any software or any preliminary settings required for the recipe.

How to do it...

This section contains the steps required to follow the recipe.

How it works...

This section usually consists of a detailed explanation of what happened in the previous section.

There's more...

This section consists of additional information about the recipe in order to make the reader more knowledgeable about the recipe.

See also

This section provides helpful links to other useful information for the recipe.

Conventions

In this book, you will find a number of text styles that distinguish between different kinds of information. Here are some examples of these styles and an explanation of their meaning.

Code words in text, database table names, folder names, filenames, file extensions, pathnames, dummy URLs, user input, and Twitter handles are shown as follows: "We can include other contexts through the use of the `include` directive."

A block of code is set as follows:

```
if (millis() - lastConnectionTime > postingInterval) {

    // Measure light level
    int sensorData = analogRead(A0);

    // Send request
    httpRequest(sensorData);
}
```

Any command-line input or output is written as follows:

```
# cp /usr/src/asterisk-addons/configs/cdr_mysql.conf.sample
  /etc/asterisk/cdr_mysql.conf
```

New terms and **important words** are shown in bold. Words that you see on the screen, for example, in menus or dialog boxes, appear in the text like this: "To do that, open the Arduino boards manager by going to **Tools** | **Boards** | **Boards Manager**."

> Warnings or important notes appear in a box like this.

> Tips and tricks appear like this.

Reader feedback

Feedback from our readers is always welcome. Let us know what you think about this book—what you liked or disliked. Reader feedback is important for us as it helps us develop titles that you will really get the most out of.

To send us general feedback, simply e-mail feedback@packtpub.com, and mention the book's title in the subject of your message.

If there is a topic that you have expertise in and you are interested in either writing or contributing to a book, see our author guide at www.packtpub.com/authors.

Customer support

Now that you are the proud owner of a Packt book, we have a number of things to help you to get the most from your purchase.

Downloading the example code

You can download the example code files for this book from your account at http://www.packtpub.com. If you purchased this book elsewhere, you can visit http://www.packtpub.com/support and register to have the files e-mailed directly to you.

You can download the code files by following these steps:

1. Log in or register to our website using your e-mail address and password.
2. Hover the mouse pointer on the **SUPPORT** tab at the top.
3. Click on **Code Downloads & Errata**.
4. Enter the name of the book in the **Search** box.

5. Select the book for which you're looking to download the code files.

6. Choose from the drop-down menu where you purchased this book from.

7. Click on **Code Download**.

You can also download the code files by clicking on the **Code Files** button on the book's webpage at the Packt Publishing website. This page can be accessed by entering the book's name in the **Search** box. Please note that you need to be logged in to your Packt account.

Once the file is downloaded, please make sure that you unzip or extract the folder using the latest version of:

- ▸ WinRAR / 7-Zip for Windows
- ▸ Zipeg / iZip / UnRarX for Mac
- ▸ 7-Zip / PeaZip for Linux

The code bundle for the book is also hosted on GitHub at `https://github.com/PacktPublishing/Internet-of-Things-with-Arduino-Cookbook`. We also have other code bundles from our rich catalog of books and videos available at `https://github.com/PacktPublishing/`. Check them out!

Errata

Although we have taken every care to ensure the accuracy of our content, mistakes do happen. If you find a mistake in one of our books—maybe a mistake in the text or the code—we would be grateful if you could report this to us. By doing so, you can save other readers from frustration and help us improve subsequent versions of this book. If you find any errata, please report them by visiting `http://www.packtpub.com/submit-errata`, selecting your book, clicking on the **Errata Submission Form** link, and entering the details of your errata. Once your errata are verified, your submission will be accepted and the errata will be uploaded to our website or added to any list of existing errata under the Errata section of that title.

To view the previously submitted errata, go to `https://www.packtpub.com/books/content/support` and enter the name of the book in the search field. The required information will appear under the **Errata** section.

Piracy

Piracy of copyrighted material on the Internet is an ongoing problem across all media. At Packt, we take the protection of our copyright and licenses very seriously. If you come across any illegal copies of our works in any form on the Internet, please provide us with the location address or website name immediately so that we can pursue a remedy.

Please contact us at copyright@packtpub.com with a link to the suspected pirated material.

We appreciate your help in protecting our authors and our ability to bring you valuable content.

Questions

If you have a problem with any aspect of this book, you can contact us at questions@ packtpub.com, and we will do our best to address the problem.

1

Connecting an Arduino to the Web

In this chapter, we will cover:

- ▸ Setting up the Arduino development environment
- ▸ Options for Internet connectivity with Arduino
- ▸ Interacting with basic sensors
- ▸ Interacting with basic actuators
- ▸ Configuring your Arduino board for the IoT
- ▸ Grabbing the content from a web page
- ▸ Sending data to the cloud
- ▸ Troubleshooting basic Arduino issues

Introduction

This first chapter of this book is focused on getting you started by connecting an Arduino board to the Web. This chapter will really be the foundation of the rest of the book, so make sure to carefully follow the instructions so you are ready to complete the exciting projects we'll see in the rest of the book.

You will first learn how to set up the Arduino IDE development environment, and add Internet connectivity to your Arduino board.

After that, we'll see how to connect a sensor and a relay to the Arduino board, for you to understand the basics of the Arduino platform. Then, we are actually going to connect an Arduino board to the Web, and use it to grab content from the Web and to store data online.

 Note that all the projects in this chapter and this book use the Arduino MKR1000 board. This is an Arduino board released in 2016 that has an on-board Wi-Fi connection. You can make all the projects in the book with other Arduino boards, but you might have to change parts of the code.

Setting up the Arduino development environment

In this first recipe of the book, we are going to see how to completely set up the Arduino IDE development environment, so that you can later use it to program your Arduino board and build Internet of Things projects.

How to do it...

The first thing you need to do is to download the latest version of the Arduino IDE from the following address:

```
https://www.arduino.cc/en/Main/Software
```

This is what you should see, and you should be able to select your operating system:

Download the Arduino Software

ARDUINO 1.6.8

The open-source Arduino Software (IDE) makes it easy to write code and upload it to the board. It runs on Windows, Mac OS X, and Linux. The environment is written in Java and based on Processing and other open-source software.
This software can be used with any Arduino board.
Refer to the Getting Started page for Installation instructions.

Windows Installer
Windows ZIP file for non admin install

Mac OS X 10.7 Lion or newer

Linux 32 bits
Linux 64 bits

Release Notes
Source Code
Checksums

You can now install the Arduino IDE, and open it on your computer. The Arduino IDE will be used through the whole book for several tasks. We will use it to write down all the code, but also to configure the Arduino boards and to read debug information back from those boards using the Arduino IDE Serial monitor.

What we need to install now is the board definition for the MKR1000 board that we are going to use in this book. To do that, open the Arduino boards manager by going to **Tools** | **Boards** | **Boards Manager**. In there, search for **SAMD boards**:

To install the board definition, just click on the little **Install** button next to the board definition.

You should now be able to select the **Arduino/GenuinoMKR1000** board inside the Arduino IDE:

You are now completely set to develop Arduino projects using the Arduino IDE and the MKR1000 board. You can, for example, try to open an example sketch inside the IDE:

```
● ● ●                          ConnectWithWPA | Arduino 1.6.8
 ⊘ ⦿ ▣ ⬆ ⬇                                                                          ◎

ConnectWithWPA                                                                      ▾

 1 /*
 2
 3  This example connects to an unencrypted Wifi network.
 4  Then it prints the  MAC address of the Wifi shield,
 5  the IP address obtained, and other network details.
 6
 7  Circuit:
 8  * WiFi shield attached|
 9
10  created 13 July 2010
11  by dlf (Metodo2 srl)
12  modified 31 May 2012
13  by Tom Igoe
14  */
15 #include <SPI.h>
16 #include <WiFi101.h>
17
18 char ssid[] = "yourNetwork";     //  your network SSID (name)
19 char pass[] = "secretPassword";  // your network password
20 int status = WL_IDLE_STATUS;     // the Wifi radio's status
21
22 void setup() {
23   //Initialize serial and wait for port to open:



 8                    Adafruit HUZZAH ESP8266, 80 MHz, 115200, 4M (3M SPIFFS) on /dev/cu.SLAB_USBtoUART
```

How it works...

The Arduino IDE is the best tool to program a wide range of boards, including the MKR1000 board that we are going to use in this book. We will see that it is a great tool to develop Internet of Things projects with Arduino. As we saw in this recipe, the board manager makes it really easy to use new boards inside the IDE.

See also

These are really the basics of the Arduino framework that we are going to use in the whole book to develop IoT projects.

Options for Internet connectivity with Arduino

Most of the boards made by Arduino don't come with Internet connectivity, which is something that we really need to build Internet of Things projects with Arduino. We are now going to review all the options that are available to us with the Arduino platform, and see which one is the best to build IoT projects.

How to do it...

The first option, which has been available since the advent of the Arduino platform, is to use a shield. A shield is basically an extension board that can be placed on top of the Arduino board. There are many shields available for Arduino. Inside the official collection of shields, you will find motor shields, prototyping shields, audio shields, and so on.

Some shields will add Internet connectivity to the Arduino boards, for example, the Ethernet shield or the Wi-Fi shield. This is an image of the Ethernet shield:

The other option is to use an external component, for example, a Wi-Fi chip mounted on a breakout board, and then connect this shield to Arduino.

There are many Wi-Fi chips available on the market. For example, Texas Instruments has a chip called the CC3000 that is really easy to connect to Arduino. This is an image of a breakout board for the CC3000 Wi-Fi chip:

Finally, there is the possibility of using one of the few Arduino boards that has an onboard Wi-Fi chip or Ethernet connectivity.

The first board of this type introduced by Arduino was the **Arduino Yun board**. It is a really powerful board, with an onboard Linux machine. However, it is also a bit complex to use compared to other Arduino boards.

Then, Arduino introduced the MKR1000 board, which is a board that integrates a powerful ARM Cortex M0+ process and a Wi-Fi chip on the same board, all in the small form factor.

Here is an image of this board:

What to choose?

All the solutions above would work to build powerful IoT projects using Arduino. However, as we want to easily build those projects and possibly integrate them into projects that are battery-powered, I chose to use the MKR1000 board for all the projects in this book.

This board is really simple to use, powerful, and doesn't require any connections to hook it up with a Wi-Fi chip. Therefore, I believe this is the perfect board for IoT projects with Arduino.

There's more...

Of course, there are other options to connect Arduino boards to the Web. One option that's becoming more and more popular is to use 3G or LTE to connect your Arduino projects to the Web, again using either shields or breakout boards. This solution has the advantage of not requiring an active Internet connection like a Wi-Fi router, and can be used anywhere, for example, outdoors.

See also

Now that we have chosen a board that we will use in our IoT projects with Arduino, you can move on to the next recipe to actually learn how to use it.

Interacting with basic sensors

In this recipe, we are going to see how to measure data coming from sensors connected to the MKR1000 board. This will really teach us the very basics of the Arduino language. As an example, we'll use a simple photocell to measure the ambient light level around the project.

Getting ready

For this project, you will need a few extra components in addition to the Arduino MKR1000 board and the usual breadboard and jumper wires:

- ▸ Photocell (https://www.sparkfun.com/products/9088)
- ▸ 10K Ohm resistor (https://www.sparkfun.com/products/8374)

We are now going to assemble the project. First, place the resistor in series with the photocell on the breadboard, next to the MKR1000 board.

Now, connect the other end of the resistor to GND on the MKR1000 board, and the other end of the photocell to the VCC pin of the Arduino board. Finally, connect the middle pin between the resistor and the photocell to analog pin A0 of the MKR1000.

This is the final result:

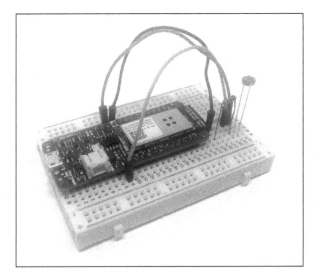

How to do it...

1. We are now going to configure the board to read data coming from the photocell. The sketch for this part will be really simple, as we will simply print the readings of analog pin A0 on the serial port. This is the complete sketch for this part:

```
// Pins
int sensorPin = A0;

void setup() {

  // Serial
  Serial.begin(115200);
}

void loop() {
  // Reading
  int sensorValue = analogRead(sensorPin);
  // Display
  Serial.print("Sensor reading: ");
  Serial.println(sensorValue);
  // Wait
  delay(500);
}
```

 You can now simply copy this sketch and paste it inside your Arduino IDE. Make sure that you connected the board to your computer via USB, and select the right board and Serial port inside the Arduino IDE. Then, upload the sketch to the board.

2. Once you have finished uploading, open the Serial monitor. You should immediately see the readings from the sensor:

```
● ○ ●                    /dev/cu.usbmodem1D11141 (Arduino/Genuino MKR1000)
                                                                      Send

Sensor reading: 636
Sensor reading: 637
Sensor reading: 277
Sensor reading: 201
Sensor reading: 187
Sensor reading: 173
Sensor reading: 161
Sensor reading: 616
Sensor reading: 636
Sensor reading: 636
Sensor reading: 636
Sensor reading: 638
Sensor reading: 636
Sensor reading: 637
Sensor reading: 637
Sensor reading: 636
Sensor reading: 637

☑ Autoscroll              Both NL & CR  ◌   115200 baud  ◌
```

3. Now, simply try to put your hand on top of the sensor. You should immediately see the value measured by the sensor coming down, meaning the sensor is working correctly.

How it works...

This project was really simple, and illustrated how to read data from an analog pin on the MKR1000 board. In this project, we simply read data on analog pin A0, and printed the readings on the Serial monitor. As the photocell is acting as a variable resistor (depending on the ambient light level), we are directly reading a signal that changes depending on the ambient light level.

See also

You can now move on to the next recipe that will show you how to control outputs on the board, or even to the recipes. After that, you will learn how to send measurement data on the cloud.

Interacting with basic actuators

In this recipe, we are now going to see how to control the outputs of the Arduino board. This will be very useful in the rest of the book, as we will control several output devices, such as lamps.

Getting ready

To realize this recipe, we first need to have something to control. Here, I will just use a simple relay, but you can of course use components, such as a single LED.

This is the relay I used for this recipe:

▸ 5V relay (https://www.pololu.com/product/2480)

We are now going to assemble the project for this recipe. First, plug the MKR1000 board into the breadboard. After that, connect the relay VCC pin to the VCC pin of the Arduino board, and the GND pin to the ground of the MKR1000. Finally, connect the SIG pin of the relay to pin 5 of the Arduino board. This is the final result:

How to do it...

1. We are now going to configure the board to see how to control outputs, like this relay. To illustrate this we are going to switch the relay on and off every second. This is the complete sketch for this recipe:

```
// Pins
int relayPin = 5;
void setup() {

  // Set pin as output
  pinMode(relayPin, OUTPUT);
}
void loop() {

  // Set relay ON
  digitalWrite(relayPin, HIGH);

  // Wait
  delay(1000);

  // Set relay OFF
  digitalWrite(relayPin, LOW);

  // Wait
  delay(1000);
}
```

2. Now, copy this sketch into the Arduino IDE and upload it to the Arduino board. Once that's done, you should immediately see (and hear) the relay switching on and off every second.

How it works...

The sketch simply uses the `digitalWrite()` function of the Arduino language to control the state of the pin to which the relay is connected, along with the `delay()` function, therefore switching the relay on and off continuously.

There's more...

You can, of course, use what you learned in this project to control other output devices, such as LEDs. We are going to see in other recipes, later in this book, how to control larger output devices, such as lamps and other home appliances.

See also

You can now continue to the next set of recipes, where we are actually going to connect the board to the Internet.

Configuring your Arduino board for the IoT

In this recipe, we are going to finally learn how to use the on-board Wi-Fi chip that is on the MKR1000 board, and connect the board to your local Wi-Fi. This is a very important recipe, are we are going to use this in nearly every recipe of this book to build IoT projects.

Getting ready

Before we can use the Wi-Fi chip that is on the board, we need an Arduino library to be able to control it. The library for this chip is called the `WiFi101` library and you can find it inside the Arduino library manager.

To access the library manager, simply go to **Sketch | Include Library | Manage Libraries** inside the Arduino IDE. Then, type `wifi101` to find the library:

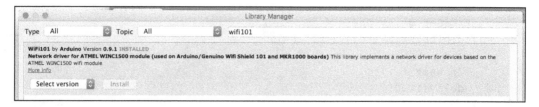

To install the library from there, simply click on the **Install** button just next to the library version.

How to do it...

Let's now connect the board to your Wi-Fi network. The sketch is quite long here, so I have split it into three parts.

This is the main part of the sketch, which will actually connect your chip to your local Wi-Fi network:

```
// Libraries
#include <SPI.h>
#include <WiFi101.h>

// Credentials
char ssid[] = "wifi-name";      //  your network SSID (name)
char pass[] = "wifi-pass";  // your network password
int status = WL_IDLE_STATUS;      // the Wifi radio's status

void setup() {

  // Serial
  Serial.begin(115200);

  // Attempt to connect to Wifi network:
  while ( status != WL_CONNECTED) {
    Serial.print("Attempting to connect to WPA SSID: ");
    Serial.println(ssid);

    // Connect to WPA/WPA2 network:
    status = WiFi.begin(ssid, pass);

    // Wait 10 seconds for connection:
    delay(10000);
  }

  // you're connected now, so print out the data:
  Serial.print("You're connected to the network");
  printCurrentNet();
  printWifiData();

}
```

```
void loop() {

    // Check the network connection once every 10 seconds:
    delay(10000);
    printCurrentNet();
}
```

What you actually need to change here are the following lines:

```
char ssid[] = "wifi-name";    //  your network SSID (name)
char pass[] = "wifi-pass";   // your network password
```

You need to change those lines to put your own Wi-Fi network's name and password. This is something you will have to do in all the sketches for the rest of this book, as we are always going to connect the Arduino board to the local Wi-Fi network.

Then, the following function will print data about your IP address:

```
void printWifiData() {
    // print your WiFi shield's IP address:
    IPAddress ip = WiFi.localIP();
    Serial.print("IP Address: ");
    Serial.println(ip);
    Serial.println(ip);

    // print your MAC address:
    byte mac[6];
    WiFi.macAddress(mac);
    Serial.print("MAC address: ");
    Serial.print(mac[5], HEX);
    Serial.print(":");
    Serial.print(mac[4], HEX);
    Serial.print(":");
    Serial.print(mac[3], HEX);
    Serial.print(":");
    Serial.print(mac[2], HEX);
    Serial.print(":");
    Serial.print(mac[1], HEX);
    Serial.print(":");
    Serial.println(mac[0], HEX);

}
```

And this function will print data about the current Wi-Fi network to which your Arduino board is connected:

```
void printCurrentNet() {
  // print the SSID of the network you're attached to:
  Serial.print("SSID: ");
  Serial.println(WiFi.SSID());

  // print the MAC address of the router you're attached to:
  byte bssid[6];
  WiFi.BSSID(bssid);
  Serial.print("BSSID: ");
  Serial.print(bssid[5], HEX);
  Serial.print(":");
  Serial.print(bssid[4], HEX);
  Serial.print(":");
  Serial.print(bssid[3], HEX);
  Serial.print(":");
  Serial.print(bssid[2], HEX);
  Serial.print(":");
  Serial.print(bssid[1], HEX);
  Serial.print(":");
  Serial.println(bssid[0], HEX);

  // print the received signal strength:
  long rssi = WiFi.RSSI();
  Serial.print("signal strength (RSSI):");
  Serial.println(rssi);

  // print the encryption type:
  byte encryption = WiFi.encryptionType();
  Serial.print("Encryption Type:");
  Serial.println(encryption, HEX);
  Serial.println();
}
```

It's now time to finally test this sketch and connect your board to the Internet! You can get the whole sketch from the GitHub repository of the following book:

```
https://github.com/marcoschwartz/iot-arduino-cookbook
```

Now, make sure to change your Wi-Fi name and password inside the sketch, and then upload the sketch to the board. Immediately open the Serial monitor. This is what you should see:

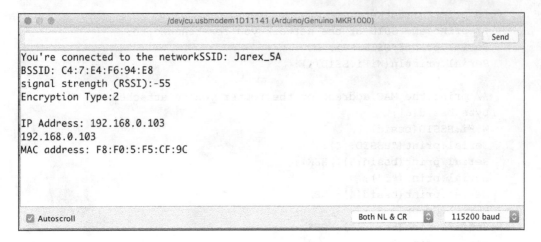

If you can see something similar, congratulations, your board is now connected to your Wi-Fi network and to the Internet (assuming your Wi-Fi router is connected to the Internet).

How it works...

The `WiFi101` library makes it really easy to use the on-board Wi-Fi chip of the MKR1000 board, and to easily connect the board to the Internet. This is a very useful function that we are going to use in the whole book.

See also

I now recommend checking the two remaining recipes in this chapter, to learn how to actually use the Internet connection of the board to interact with web services.

Grabbing the content from a web page

To illustrate how the `WiFi101` library is working on the MKR1000 board, we are now going to use it to grab the content of a web page, and display the result inside the Serial monitor.

Getting ready

You do not need any extra steps here, simply make sure that you have the `WiFi101` library installed.

How to do it...

Let's now see the sketch for this recipe. As it is really similar to the sketch of the previous recipe, I will only highlight the main pieces of code that were added here:

1. You first need to define which page we are going to grab. Here, I will just make the board grab the `www.example.com` page:

```
char server[] = "www.example.com";
```

2. Then, we need to create an instance of a Wi-Fi client:

```
WiFiClient client;
```

3. Then, inside the `setup()` function of the sketch, we connect to the server we defined earlier, and request the Web page:

```
// Connect to server
  if (client.connect(server, 80)) {
    Serial.println("connected to server");

    // Make a request:
    client.println("GET / HTTP/1.1");
    client.println("Host: www.example.com");
    client.println("Connection: close");
    client.println();
  }
```

4. Inside the `loop()` function of the sketch, we then read the data coming back from the server, and print it inside the Serial port:

```
while (client.available()) {
    char c = client.read();
    Serial.write(c);
  }
```

5. We then stop the connection with the following piece of code:

```
// Stop the connection
  if (!client.connected()) {
    Serial.println();
    Serial.println("disconnecting from server.");
    client.stop();

    // do nothing forevermore:
    while (true);
}
```

6. It's now time to try this sketch! First, grab the code from the GitHub repository of this book, and then change your Wi-Fi credentials inside the code. Then, upload the code to the board, and open the Serial monitor. This is what you should see:

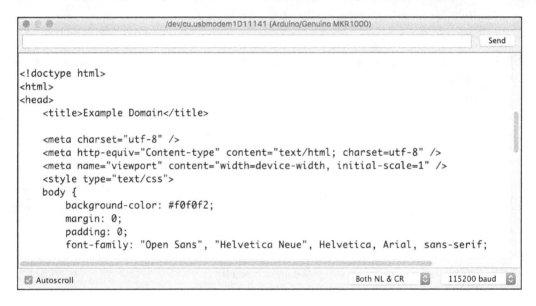

If you can see that, it means that the board has successfully grabbed the content of the web page and displayed it inside the Serial monitor.

How it works...

The sketch uses the Wi-Fi client of the `WiFi101` library, which is a very powerful object that we will use again in several chapters of this book.

See also

I now recommend checking the next recipe, in which you will actually learn how to use the Wi-Fi client library to send data to a cloud server.

Sending data to the cloud

In the last recipe of this chapter, we are actually going to use everything we learned so far in this chapter and apply it to a simple project: sending data to a cloud server, so it can be stored there. This is something that we are going to do many times in this book, but I wanted to give you a short overview first.

Getting ready

For this recipe, you will need the same configuration that we used in the recipe *Interacting with basic sensors*, but ? with a photocell connected to the Arduino board. Please refer to this recipe to know how to assemble the hardware for the project.

How to do it...

Let's now see the sketch that we will use for this chapter. It is actually very similar to the code for the previous chapter, so I will just highlight the important parts here.

As before, we define the server to which we want to connect the board. Here, we will use the dweet.io service:

```
char server[] = "dweet.io";
```

We also define an interval on which we will send data to the dweet.io servers:

```
unsigned long lastConnectionTime = 0;
const unsigned long postingInterval = 10L * 1000L;
```

In the loop() function, we check if it is time to send data. If so, we measure the reading from the sensor, and send this to a function that will send the data:

```
    if (millis() - lastConnectionTime > postingInterval) {

        // Measure light level
        int sensorData = analogRead(A0);

        // Send request
        httpRequest(sensorData);
    }
```

Let's now see the details of this function:

```
    void httpRequest(int sensorData) {

      // Close existing connection
      client.stop();

      // Connect & send request
      if (client.connect(server, 80)) {

        Serial.println("connecting...");

        // Send the HTTP PUT request:
        client.println("GET /dweet/for/myarduino?light=" +
    String(sensorData) + " HTTP/1.1");
        client.println("Host: dweet.io");
        client.println("User-Agent: ArduinoWiFi/1.1");
        client.println("Connection: close");
        client.println();

        // Note the time that the connection was made:
        lastConnectionTime = millis();
      }
      else {
        // if you couldn't make a connection:
        Serial.println("connection failed");
      }
    }
```

As you can see, the function is very similar to what we did in the previous recipe. The main difference is that we pass the measured data as an argument when calling the `dweet.io` server.

You can now grab the code from the GitHub repository of this book, and upload it to the board.

 Don't forget to change your Wi-Fi name and password here, otherwise it won't work.

Then, open the Serial monitor, and this is what you should see:

```
●●●                    /dev/cu.usbmodem1D11141 (Arduino/Genuino MKR1000)

                                                                        Send
SSID: Jarex_5A
IP Address: 192.168.0.103
signal strength (RSSI):-54 dBm
connecting...
HTTP/1.1 200 OK
Access-Control-Allow-Origin: *
Content-Type: application/json
Content-Length: 193
Date: Mon, 02 May 2016 17:17:46 GMT
Connection: close

{"this":"succeeded","by":"dweeting","the":"dweet","with":{"thing":"myarduino","created":"2016-05-
HTTP/1.1 200 OK
Access-Control-Allow-Origin: *
Content-Type: application/json
Content-Length: 193
Date: Mon, 02 May 2016 17:17:56 GMT
Connection: close

{"this":"succeeded","by":"dweeting","the":"dweet","with":{"thing":"myarduino","created":"2016-05-

☐ Autoscroll                              Both NL & CR ⬍   115200 baud ⬍
```

If you can see the **'succeeded'** message, it means that the data has been correctly stored on the server.

To check that it was actually recorded, you can now go to the following URL:

`https://dweet.io/get/latest/dweet/for/myarduino`

You should see the answer in JSON format, meaning data was recorded from your board.

```
←  →  C  🔒 https://dweet.io/get/latest/dweet/for/myarduino
{"this":"succeeded","by":"getting","the":"dweets","with":[{"thing":"myarduino","created":"2016-05-02T17:18:26.985Z","content":{"light":299}}]}
```

How it works...

The Dweet.io service is a very useful (and free) web service to store data coming from your IoT project. We are going to use it extensively in the coming chapters of this book.

See also

I now recommend that you move on to the next chapter, so you can start using what you learned in this introductory chapter to build actual IoT projects!

Troubleshooting basic Arduino issues

In this part of the chapter, we are going to see what can go wrong when configuring your board and connecting it to the Internet. Indeed, some of the steps involved here are quite complex and many things can go differently than expected.

The board is not visible from the Arduino IDE

The first thing that can happen is that the board is not visible from the Arduino IDE, even if you have it connected to your computer via USB. Make sure that you are using a data USB cable: many cables nowadays are just for charging and don't actually allow data transfers. If you are using Windows, also make sure to refer to the Arduino website to install the required drivers.

The board doesn't connect to your Wi-Fi router

If you can't connect the board to your local Wi-Fi router, make sure that you correctly entered your Wi-Fi name and password inside the sketch before uploading it to the board. The sketches of this book are made for WPA Wi-Fi networks, which are most of the networks out there. However, if you are still using a WEP network, make sure to check the Arduino WiFi101 example sketches to learn how to connect the board to a WEP network.

Cloud Data Monitoring

2

In this chapter, we will cover:

- ► Internet of Things platforms for Arduino
- ► Connecting sensors to your Arduino board
- ► Posting the sensor data online
- ► Retrieving your online data
- ► Monitoring sensor data from a cloud dashboard
- ► Monitoring several Arduino boards at once
- ► Troubleshooting issues with cloud data monitoring

Introduction

One of the most important things you can do with an Internet of Things project is to send data online, so it can be stored, retrieved later, and plotted inside a nice dashboard. Of course, it needs to be accessible from any web browser or application in the world.

In this chapter, this is exactly what we are going to do with Arduino. We are going to use an Arduino board to log sensor data online, and then we'll see how to exploit this data. We are first going to get an overview of what options are available when you want to log data online from an Arduino project. Then, we are going to connect sensors to the Arduino board, and log this data online. Finally, we'll see how to access this data, plot it, and also visualize data coming from several boards at once.

Internet of Things platforms for Arduino

In the first recipe of this chapter, we are going to see the different platforms that are available for us, if we want to store data online from an Arduino project. We'll see what are the strengths and the weaknesses of each platform, so we can make a choice for the rest of this chapter.

Available platforms

The first platform that I wanted to mention here is called Dweet.io. You can learn more about it at:

```
https://dweet.io/
```

Dweet.io is basically a simple API that can be called from any web browser or application, and it is so simple to use that even a human can use it without problems! It's really easy to store data there from an Arduino project, and then to retrieve this data using other applications.

The next platform I wanted to mention here is Xively. This is the main page of Xively:

```
https://xively.com/
```

Xively is a complete IoT platform, which is more dedicated to the business world than Dweet. io, for example. It includes more functions than just storage of data – for example, you can plot data right on their platform as well.

The next platform is called **Adafruit IO.** You can access the platform by going to the following URL:

```
https://io.adafruit.com/
```

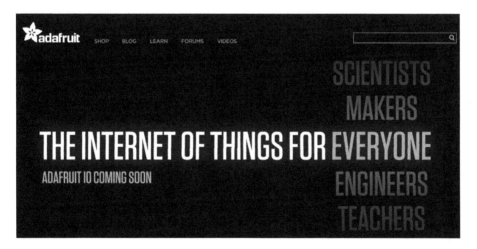

Made by the manufacturer of the Adafruit open source hardware products, the platform was made to be really easy to use with Adafruit products and libraries, for example, their ESP8266 breakout boards, and their FONA product line that connects to the Internet via GPRS or 3G. At the time of writing, the service was still in open beta.

The last cloud service I want to mention in this recipe is the SparkFun data service, accessible from:

```
https://data.sparkfun.com/
```

This service is relatively similar to Dweet.io, and allows the user to easily store data online. You will also find a lot of tutorials showing you how to use this service with SparkFun products. For this chapter, and most of this book, I decided to use Dweet.io to store data online, as it is the easiest solution when using an Arduino board.

How it works...

All these services work in a similar fashion – you need to call the API of this service, with the data that you want to store online. This will be done by the Arduino board in the recipes in this chapter, where we will send sensor data to those services.

Then, we will be able to use this data from other services, for example, to plot the data graphically inside online dashboards.

There's more...

There are, of course, other platforms that are available out there to store data online, and that are also easy to use from Arduino boards. You are, of course, free to use the platform that you wish, you will simply need to adapt the code that you will find in the different recipes of this book.

See also

As this is the simplest cloud storage service of this recipe, we are mainly going to use the Dweet.io website in the recipes in this chapter. Therefore, I recommend that you move to the next recipe to see how to connect sensors to the Arduino board.

Connecting sensors to your Arduino board

In this recipe, we are going to build the project that we will use for the rest of this chapter. We basically want to connect sensors to the Arduino MKR1000 board that will continuously measure data. As an example here, we are going to connect a photocell (that we already used in the first chapter of this book), as well as a DHT11 temperature and humidity sensor.

Getting ready

Let's first see what additional components we will need for this project:

- Photocell (`https://www.sparkfun.com/products/9088`)
- 10K Ohm resistor (`https://www.sparkfun.com/products/8374`)
- DHT11 sensor (`https://www.adafruit.com/products/386`)

You will also need to install the Adafruit DHT library that you can find inside the Arduino board manager.

We are now going to assemble the project. First, place the resistor in series with the photocell on the breadboard, next to the MKR1000 board.

Now, connect the other end of the resistor to GND on the MKR1000 board, and the other end of the photocell to the VCC pin of the Arduino board. Finally, connect the middle pin between the resistor and the photocell to analog pin A0 of the MKR1000.

To connect the DHT11 sensor, place it on the board as well. Then, connect the first pin of the sensor to VCC, the second pin to pin 5 of the Arduino board, and then the last pin of the sensor to GND.

This is the final result:

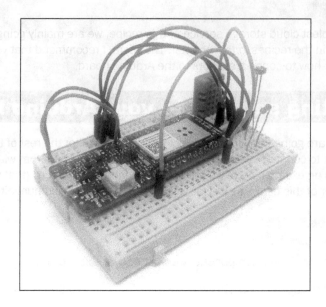

This is the completely assembled project from another angle:

How to do it...

We are now going to write some code to test the sensors. This will make sure that we have connected everything correctly, before we move on to the next step that sends the data to a cloud service:

1. First, we need to include the DHT library:

   ```
   #include "DHT.h"
   ```

2. Then, we define the pins on which the sensors are connected, and we declare the type of the DHT sensor:

   ```
   int sensorPin = A0;
   #define DHTPIN 5
   #define DHTTYPE DHT11
   ```

3. We also need to create an instance of the DHT sensor:

   ```
   DHT dht(DHTPIN, DHTTYPE, 15);
   ```

4. Inside the `setup()` function of the sketch, we initialize the DHT sensor:

   ```
   dht.begin();
   ```

5. In the `loop()` function of the sketch, we first read data from the DHT sensor, and print it inside the Serial monitor:

   ```
   // Reading temperature and humidity
     float humidity = dht.readHumidity();
     // Read temperature as Celsius
     float temperature = dht.readTemperature();

     // Display
     Serial.print("Temperature: ");
     Serial.print(temperature);
     Serial.println(" C");

     Serial.print("Humidity: ");
     Serial.print(humidity);
     Serial.println(" %");
   ```

6. We then do the same for the photocell:

```
// Reading from analog sensor
  int sensorValue = analogRead(sensorPin);
  float lightLevel = sensorValue/1024.*100;
  // Display
  Serial.print("Light level: ");
  Serial.print(lightLevel);
  Serial.println(" %");
  Serial.println();
```

7. It's now time to test the project! Grab all the code from the GitHub repository of the project at: `https://github.com/marcoschwartz/iot-arduino-cookbook`.

8. Then, upload the code to the board, and open the Serial monitor. This is what you should see:

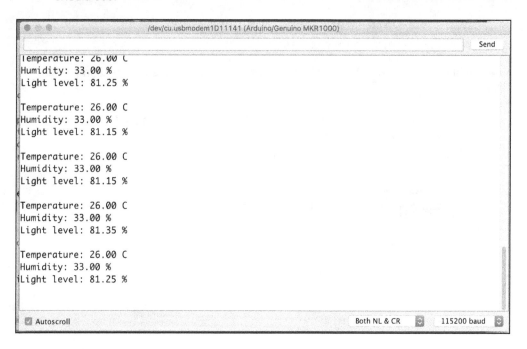

Congratulations, if you can see that, you can now read data from sensors connected to your MKR1000 board!

How it works...

In this recipe, we introduced a new kind of sensor with the DHT11: digital sensors. These types of sensors usually work along with a dedicated library (for example, for Arduino), and are quite easy to use. As you can see in this recipe, we were able to easily measure the temperature and humidity within the code.

There's more...

You can, of course, connect other sensors to your Arduino board: the two sensors I used in this project were just examples, to have some data to log to a cloud service. You could, for example, use a barometric pressure sensor, an accelerometer, a gyroscope, and so on.

See also

To now see how to actually use this data and log it inside a cloud service, I recommend following the next recipe of this chapter.

Posting the sensor data online

Using the Arduino MKR1000 board and the sensors that we connected to it, we are finally going to log data online, using the Dweet.io service.

Getting ready

For this recipe, you simply need to have the previous recipe up and running, so make sure you have all the sensors connected to your board, and that you have tested them with the test sketch.

You should already have it by now, but make sure that you have the Arduino `WiFi101` library installed inside the Arduino IDE.

How to do it...

We are now going to configure the board so it sends the measurements from the sensor to Dweet.io at regular intervals. As this sketch is quite similar to what we already saw in previous chapters, I will only highlight the most important parts of the code here:

1. First, we need to define the libraries that we are going to use in this project:

```
#include <SPI.h>
#include <WiFi101.h>
#include "DHT.h"
```

2. Then, we need to define a name for our thing on Dweet.io, which is the name we will use to retrieve the data later:

```
char * thingName = "mymkr1000";
```

3. Then, inside the `loop()` function of the sketch, we make measurements from the sensors at regular intervals, and then we send this data to the server:

```
if (millis() - lastConnectionTime > postingInterval) {

    // Reading temperature and humidity
    float humidity = dht.readHumidity();

    // Read temperature as Celsius
    float temperature = dht.readTemperature();

    // Reading from analog sensor
    int sensorValue = analogRead(sensorPin);
    float lightLevel = sensorValue/1024.*100;

    // Send request
    httpRequest(temperature, humidity, lightLevel);
}
```

4. We already saw the `httpRequest()` function in a previous recipe, so I will let you discover it inside the code itself.

5. It's now time to finally test the project!

Make sure to grab all the code from the GitHub repository of this book, and modify your Wi-Fi name and password inside the code. Also make sure to modify the name of your 'thing' as I used quite a generic name.

6. Then, upload the code to the board, and open the Serial monitor. It looks something like this:

```
/dev/cu.usbmodem1D11141 (Arduino/Genuino MKR1000)                          Send

connecting...
HTTP/1.1 200 OK
Access-Control-Allow-Origin: *
Content-Type: application/json
Content-Length: 226
Date: Fri, 06 May 2016 09:34:27 GMT
Connection: close

{"this":"succeeded","by":"dweeting","the":"dweet","with":{"thing":"mymkr1000","created":"2016-05-06T09:34:27.937Z"
HTTP/1.1 200 OK
Access-Control-Allow-Origin: *
Content-Type: application/json
Content-Length: 226
Date: Fri, 06 May 2016 09:34:38 GMT
Connection: close

{"this":"succeeded","by":"dweeting","the":"dweet","with":{"thing":"mymkr1000","created":"2016-05-06T09:34:38.475Z"
HTTP/1.1 200 OK
Access-Control-Allow-Origin: *
Content-Type: application/json

Autoscroll                                        Both NL & CR      115200 baud
```

The important part of the output is the following:

```
',"content":{"temperature":26,"humidity":33,"light":69.24},"
```

Those numbers are our measurements, and if you can see them it means that your measurements have been stored on the Dweet.io server!

How it works...

The sketch simply sends all the measurements to the Dweet.io server via a CIT12 request. The information is then stored there in JSON format, which is what we see inside the output.

See also

Storing data online is good, but what we really want to do is to reuse it later. This is why you can now move on to the next couple of recipes in this chapter.

Retrieving your online data

Now that we have stored measurement data in the previous recipe, we are now going to learn how to retrieve it and possibly use it inside applications.

Getting ready

For this recipe, you need to have some data stored on the Dweet.io server. For that, please follow the previous recipe if that's not done yet.

How to do it...

Let's suppose that you have data stored for a device called "mymkr1000" on the Dweet. io server. You can easily access the latest data that was stored on the server by typing the following command inside any web browser:

```
https://dweet.io/get/latest/dweet/for/mymkr1000
```

This will be the result:

```
{
    "this":"succeeded",
    "by":"getting",
    "the":"dweets",
    "with":[
        {
            "thing":"mymkr1000",
            "created":"2016-05-06T09:35:31.110Z",
            "content":{
                "temperature":26,
                "humidity":33,
                "light":71.97
            }
        }
    ]
}
```

As you can see, the server returns the latest `datapoint` that was stored for this device, in the form of a JSON document.

To get all the data that was stored for this device, you can type:

```
https://dweet.io/get/dweets/for/mymkr1000
```

You should get a result similar to this:

```
{
    "this":"succeeded",
    "by":"getting",
    "the":"dweets",
    "with":[
        {
            "thing":"mymkr1000",
            "created":"2016-05-06T09:50:19.635Z",
            "content":{
                "temperature":26,
                "humidity":33,
                "light":79.1
            }
        },
        {
            "thing":"mymkr1000",
            "created":"2016-05-06T09:50:09.124Z",
            "content":{
                "temperature":26,
                "humidity":33,
                "light":79.1
            }
        },
        {
            "thing":"mymkr1000",
            "created":"2016-05-06T09:49:59.473Z",
            "content":{
                "temperature":26,
                "humidity":33,
                "light":78.91
            }
        },
        {
```

```
        "thing":"mymkr1000",
        "created":"2016-05-06T09:49:48.089Z",
        "content":{
            "temperature":26,
            "humidity":33,
            "light":79.39
        }
    },
    {
        "thing":"mymkr1000",
        "created":"2016-05-06T09:49:37.594Z",
        "content":{
            "temperature":26,
            "humidity":33,
            "light":79.59
        }
    }
    ]
}
```

Here, the result is returned as a JSON array, which contains the data stored by this 'thing' on Dweet.io.

How it works...

The Dweet.io service can also be used to easily retrieve data that was stored on the device, via a simple HTTP request. You can now use this data for your information only, or inside your own web applications.

See also

If you now want to protect your stored data, you can have a look at the next recipe. Otherwise, you can skip the next recipe and just go to the next one in which we'll learn how to plot the data that is stored on Dweet.io.

Securing your online data

We are now going to learn how to protect the data that was stored by your devices. Indeed, using the recipes we saw so far, anyone can log data to your devices and then retrieve this data via a simple web request.

Getting ready

The key to protecting your data stored on Dweet.io is to use locks. You can learn more about locks at:

```
https://dweet.io/locks
```

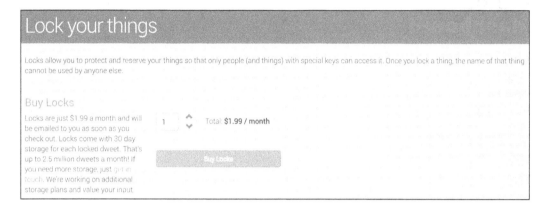

Basically, you can buy a lock to protect your devices, and then to access them or log new data you will need to always provide the key associated with this lock.

How to do it...

The first step is to lock the device, which is done by calling the URL, passing your thing name, lock, and key:

```
https://dweet.io/lock/{thing_name}?lock={your_lock}&key={your_key}
```

To actually log data to a device protected by a lock, you need to provide the lock and the key whenever you are calling the API from the Arduino board. For example:

```
https://dweet.io/dweet/for/{my_locked_thing}?key={my_
key}&hello=world&foo=bar
```

The same is then necessary to retrieve data from this device.

How it works...

Locks can be used to prevent anyone from accessing one of your 'things' on the Dweet.io service – you then need a key to perform any operation on the device. This is particularly useful if you have sensitive data that you don't want anybody else to access.

See also

I now recommend checking the remaining recipes of this chapter, to learn how to plot the stored data graphically inside a cloud dashboard.

Monitoring sensor data from a cloud dashboard

So far in this chapter, we stored data on Dweet.io, and we also saw how to retrieve the data back from the server. However, what would be even better is to learn how to plot this data inside a dashboard that is also in the cloud. And that's exactly what we are going to do in this recipe.

Getting ready

For this recipe, you will need to have an account with Freeboard.io, which is a very convenient service that you can use to plot data graphically. To do so, just go to:

`http://freeboard.io/`

Now, inside the Freeboard.io interface, create a new dashboard:

My Freeboards	MKR1000	Create New

You should also make sure that the project we used in previous recipes is still running, and still logging data on Dweet.io.

How to do it...

Now, go to your newly created panel inside `http://freeboard.io/`. Next, click on **DATASOURCES** to create a new source of data:

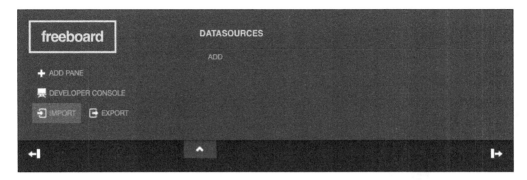

Inside, you need to select **Dweet.io** as the type of the data source, and you also need to put the name of your thing **Dweet.io**:

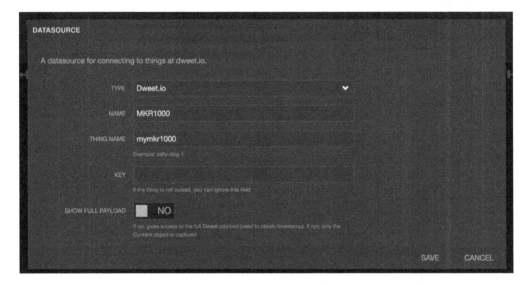

The newly created data source should now appear inside the dashboard:

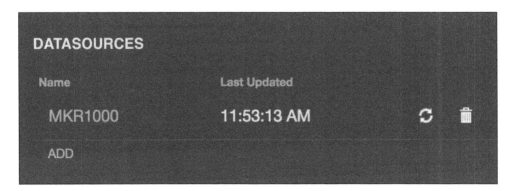

Now that you have a data source inside the dashboard, it's time to actually plot the data in it. For that, first create a new panel, and inside this panel add a new element.

To display our data here, we are going to add gauges. These are the parameters for the temperature gauge:

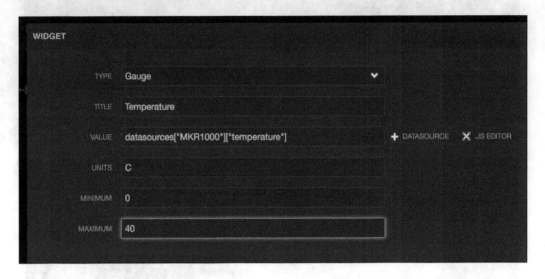

You can now do the same for the humidity and the light level. At the end, you should have a dashboard with three different gauges:

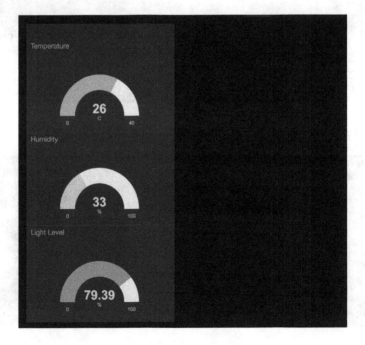

How it works...

Freeboard.io allows you to easily plot the data stored on Dweet.io inside a dashboard. Because the dashboard is also on a web server, your data is accessible from anywhere, and you can even share your dashboards with your friends so they too can visualize the data coming from your projects.

See also

In order to continue building cloud dashboards, I recommend checking the last recipe of this chapter where we will actually integrate several boards inside the same dashboard.

Monitoring several Arduino boards at once

In the last recipe of this chapter, we are going to see how to integrate the data coming from several Arduino boards at once inside the same dashboard, so you can monitor all your data from a single place, wherever you are on the planet.

Getting ready

For this recipe, you will need to have already released22 the project from the previous recipe, and have a project logging data on Dweet.io, and linked to Freeboard.io as well.

Then, you can build as many of those projects as you want, with the same components on each project. For this recipe, I used three MKR1000 boards, each with the same sensors.

How to do it...

You can now program all of your boards. You can use the same code that we used earlier in this chapter, but for each device you need to change the name of the 'thing' on Dweet.io. For example:

```
char * thingName = "mymkr1000_two";
```

Next, inside `http://Freeboard.io`, you need to set a new data source for each board you have in your project, with the respective 'thing' name:

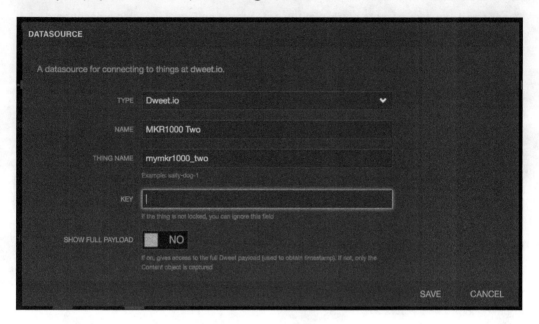

You will now have several data sources in your dashboard:

Next, for each new data source, add new gauge widgets, by selecting the correct data source inside the widget:

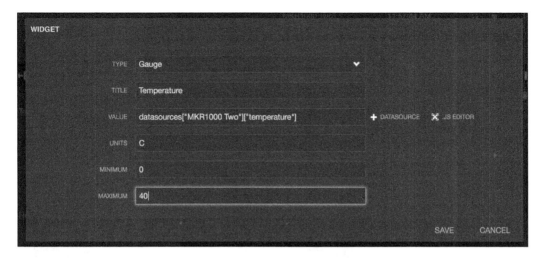

If you do that for all measurements and for all boards (I had three when I tested the project), you will end up with a dashboard similar to this one:

How it works...

Freeboard.io allows you to add several data sources inside the same dashboard, so it is really easy to display the measurements coming from several Arduino boards inside the same cloud dashboard.

There's more...

You can, of course, add many more than three boards inside your project! You can also, for example, mix the sensors, by having some boards' measure only the temperature and humidity, and other boards measuring other parameters.

See also

I now recommend checking the troubleshooting section in case you had any problems with this chapter.

Troubleshooting issues with cloud data monitoring

In this part of the chapter, we are going to see what can go wrong when logging data to a cloud service, and displaying this data inside a dashboard:

- **The board can't connect to Dweet.io**: The first thing that can happen is that the board has no Internet connection. Enter the correct Wi-Fi name and password inside the sketch. Also make sure that your router has an active Internet connection. Finally, make sure that the sensors are correctly reading values in the sketch, as it could corrupt the data sent to Dweet.io.

- **The results are not visible inside the**: If the results are not showing up inside the cloud dashboard, first make sure that your device is correctly logging data on Dweet.io. Also make sure that you entered the correct name for your 'thing' on Freeboard.io.

3
Interacting with Web Services

In this chapter, we will cover:

- ▶ Discovering the Temboo platform
- ▶ Tweeting from an Arduino board
- ▶ Posting updates on Facebook
- ▶ Storing data on Google Drive
- ▶ Automation with IFTTT
- ▶ Sending push notifications
- ▶ Sending text message notifications
- ▶ Troubleshooting usual issues with web services

Introduction

Having an Arduino board that can easily be connected to the Internet allows many exciting applications, for example, by making the board communicate with existing web services.

In this chapter, we are going to learn how to use existing web services to really build amazing Internet of Things projects with our Arduino board. We'll, for example, use it to post on Facebook or Twitter, and to send automated notifications based on data measured by the board.

Discovering the Temboo platform

To interact with web services from the Arduino MKR1000 board, the easiest thing to do is to use a platform that will make the connection between the board and the web services themselves.

The first platform of this kind that we are going to use in this chapter is the Temboo platform, which was the platform recommended by Arduino when their first IoT product (the Arduino Yun) came out. We'll see how easy it is to create an account there and how to use it to connect to a lot of web services.

Getting ready

1. The first step is to create a Temboo account. To do so, simply visit `https://temboo.com/`.

2. You should then be able to create an account and log in:

3. After that, you will be able to explore the Temboo libraries to interact with other web services, which are called Choreos:

4. You can now click on a given Choreo to see what kinds of interactions are available. For example, this is the Disqus Choreo:

5. For example, this is what you will see if you click on one possible interaction:

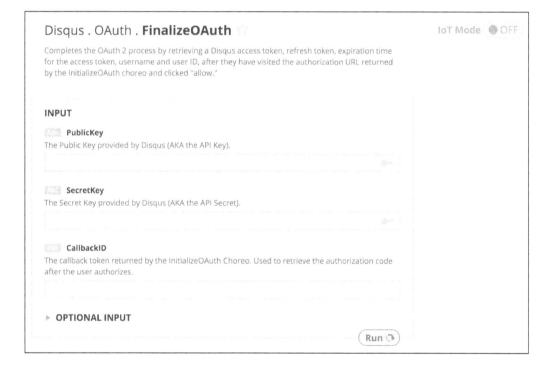

How it works...

Temboo works by making the link between your Arduino boards (or other boards/applications) and web services such as Twitter, Facebook, Dropbox, and so on. It is then very easy to use all those services from your own applications and projects.

There's more...

You can now already that time to explore the available Choreos, and see what you could use in your projects involving the Arduino board.

See also

I now recommend moving on to the next recipe to learn how to use Temboo to tweet from your Arduino board.

Tweeting from an Arduino board

In this recipe, we are going to learn how to use Temboo to tweet a message from your Arduino board. We are going to create an app on Twitter, and then see how to configure your Arduino board to send tweets from it.

Getting ready

1. The first step is to create a Twitter account if that's not done yet, and then log in with this account at `https://apps.twitter.com/`.

2. You will then be able to create a Twitter application:

Application Details

Name *

```
MKR1000
```

Your application name. This is used to attribute the source of a tweet and in user-facing authorization screens. 32 characters max.

Description *

```
Sending tweets from MKR1000
```

Your application description, which will be shown in user-facing authorization screens. Between 10 and 200 characters max.

Website *

```
http://example.com/
```

Your application's publicly accessible home page, where users can go to download, make use of, or find out more information about your application. This fully-qualified URL is used in the source attribution for tweets created by your application and will be shown in user-facing authorization screens.

(If you don't have a URL yet, just put a placeholder here but remember to change it later.)

Callback URL

```

```

Where should we return after successfully authenticating? OAuth 1.0a applications should explicitly specify their oauth_callback URL on the request token step, regardless of the value given here. To restrict your application from using callbacks, leave this field blank.

---

3. What matters is to get the application API key and app secret:

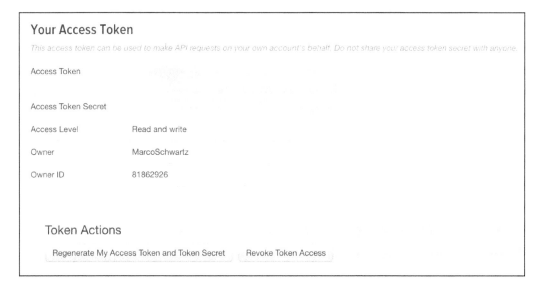

4. You will also have to get the app access token and token secret:

How to do it...

Let's now see how to configure the Arduino board. You have two choices here: either do it from the Temboo interface, or simply grab the sketch from the GitHub repository of the project.

As Temboo does not officially support the MKR1000 board at the time of writing, I recommend getting the code from the GitHub repository of this book.

The Choreo we are going to use here is called **statusesUpdate**:

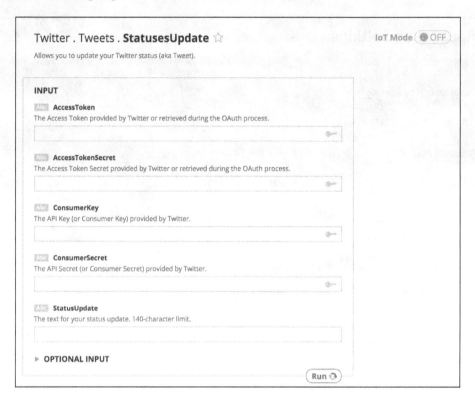

Let's now see how to configure the Arduino board. As the code is quite long, I will only highlight the main parts here. It starts by including the required libraries and files:

```
#include <SPI.h>
#include <WiFi101.h>
#include <Temboo.h>
#include "TembooAccount.h" // Contains Temboo account information
```

Then we configure the Twitter Choreo with the message that we want to Tweet, along with the API key and secret, and the token and token secret:

```
// Set Choreo inputs
    String StatusUpdateValue = "Hello from Arduino!";
    StatusesUpdateChoreo.addInput("StatusUpdate", StatusUpdateValue);
    String ConsumerKeyValue = "key";
    StatusesUpdateChoreo.addInput("ConsumerKey", ConsumerKeyValue);
    String AccessTokenValue = "token";
    StatusesUpdateChoreo.addInput("AccessToken", AccessTokenValue);
    String ConsumerSecretValue = "secret";
```

```
    StatusesUpdateChoreo.addInput("ConsumerSecret",
ConsumerSecretValue);
    String AccessTokenSecretValue = "secretToken";
    StatusesUpdateChoreo.addInput("AccessTokenSecret",
AccessTokenSecretValue);
```

Finally, the `Temboo.h` file contains all the data relative to your Temboo account:

```
#define TEMBOO_ACCOUNT "account"   // Your Temboo account name
#define TEMBOO_APP_KEY_NAME "app"  // Your Temboo app key name
#define TEMBOO_APP_KEY "key"  // Your Temboo app key
```

You can now grab the whole code from the GitHub repository of this book at `https://github.com/marcoschwartz/iot-arduino-cookbook`.

Inside this sketch, you need to modify the Wi-Fi name and password, the Twitter credentials, and also your Temboo credentials inside the `.h` file. Once that's done, you can upload the file to the board.

Then, open your Twitter feed. You should shortly see the status update that you defined in the code appear on your feed:

Marco Schwartz @MarcoSchwartz · 6s

Hello from Arduino!

Congratulations, you can now tweet from your Arduino board!

How it works...

The project works by making the Arduino MKR1000 board talk with the Temboo servers. Temboo then makes sure to authenticate with your Twitter application, which then posts on your Twitter account.

See also

For a variation of this recipe, I recommend moving to the next one in which you will learn to post updates via Facebook.

Posting updates on Facebook

In this recipe, we are going to learn how to use Temboo again, this time to post an update on your Facebook feed.

Getting ready

1. The first step is to create a Facebook application. To do so, go to `https://developers.facebook.com/`.

2. You will then be able to name your app:

3. Then you need to add the following line inside the settings of your app, replacing `account_name` with the name of your Temboo account:

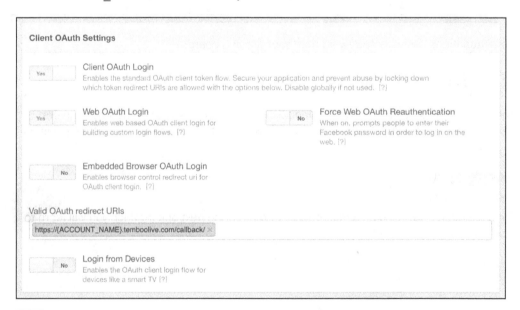

4. Now we need to authorize the use of this application by the Temboo servers. To do so, visit `https://temboo.com/library/Library/Facebook/OAuth/InitializeOAuth/`.

5. Here you will need to insert the application ID, which can be found on the Facebook app page:

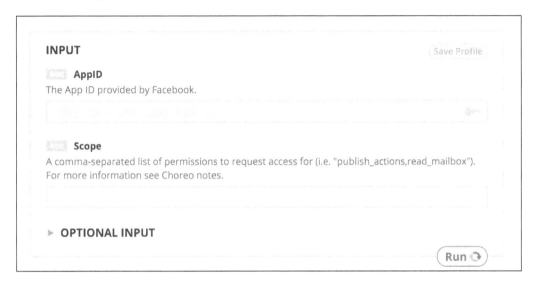

6. Once that's done, you will need to visit a URL to authorize the app:

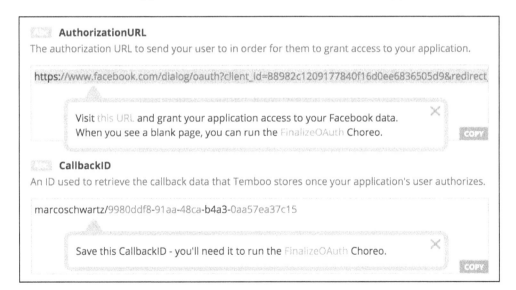

7. Finally, after following all the steps from the Temboo website, you will be given your access token that will be used by the Arduino board to post on Facebook:

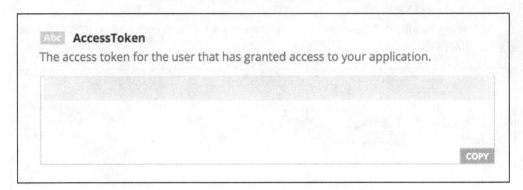

How to do it...

For the rest of this recipe, we'll use the Choreo at `https://temboo.com/library/Library/Facebook/Publishing/Post/`.

This will allow the application to post on your Facebook profile feed. As the sketch is really similar to the one of the previous, I will only highlight the main difference here, which is the part of the sketch where you define the message to post on Facebook and the access token:

```
String MessageValue = "Hello from Arduino";
PostChoreo.addInput("Message", MessageValue);
String AccessTokenValue = "token";
PostChoreo.addInput("AccessToken", AccessTokenValue);
```

▶ You can now grab the code from the GitHub repository of this book, and modify your Wi-Fi credentials, add the Facebook access token you got from Temboo, and finally also modify the `Temboo.h` file with your Temboo credentials.

▶ Then, upload the code to the Arduino board. You should see that quickly after that, you will see the message you defined in the code appear on your Facebook feed.

How it works...

Just like the previous recipe, this project uses the Temboo platform to make the link between the Arduino board and the Facebook servers, to post automatically on Facebook using the Arduino board.

See also

I now recommend exploring the next recipes of this chapter, to learn how to use other web services.

Automation with IFTTT

In the next few recipes of this book, we are going to use another website to interact with web services: IFTTT. We'll see how IFTTT will allow you to quickly define powerful automation rules and actions that can be triggered by the Arduino board.

Getting ready

The first step for all the remaining recipes of this chapter is to create an IFTTT account at `https://ifttt.com`.

From there, you will be able to explore the first important part of IFTTT: channels. Channels are all the web services or triggers that you can use within IFTTT, for example, Gmail, Twitter, Pushover, and so on. You can quickly have an overview of the available channels:

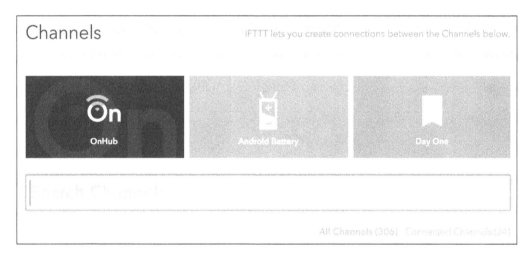

For example, if you type `Weather`, you can quickly add the weather channel, allowing you to trigger actions depending on the weather:

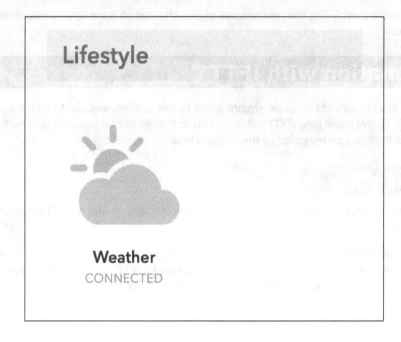

The next important part of IFTTT is recipes. Recipes allow the user to create an action (on a given channel) when a trigger is called (on another channel). This is really the core of IFTTT. You can also quickly browse the already existing library of recipes on IFTTT:

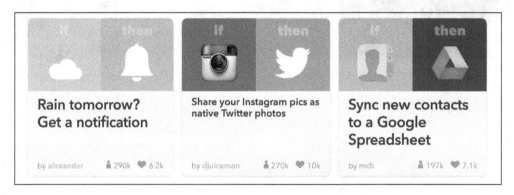

However, for our projects, we are mostly going to create our own recipes. And for that, we need to connect a very important channel to our account: the **Maker channel**. This will allow the Arduino board to communicate with the IFTTT servers.

To connect with this channel, search for **Maker**:

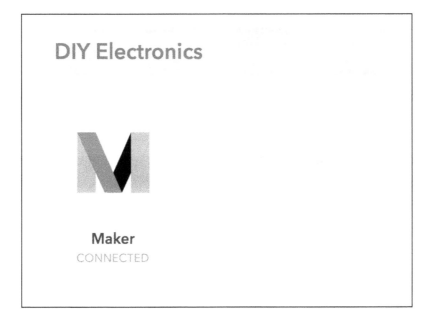

Once the channel is added, you will get a key that we will use in all the remaining projects of this chapter:

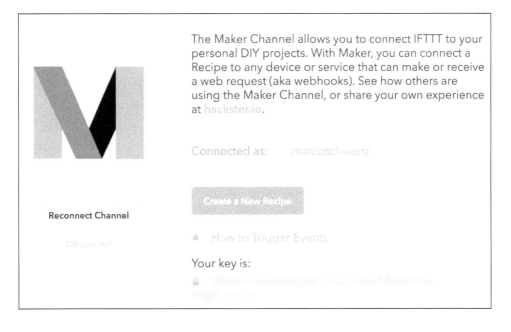

There's more...

You can now take some time to explore all the channels that are available on IFTTT, and think about how to use them in your Arduino IoT projects.

See also

I now recommend moving to the next recipe, in which we will use IFTTT to send push notifications.

Sending push notifications

In this recipe, we are going to see how to send push notifications from your Arduino boards, via IFTTT. As we are slowly discovering the IFTTT service, we are only going to build a simple alert system here.

Getting ready

To start, you need to connect to the **Pushover** channel, which is a service to send notifications to your mobile device. If you don't have a **Pushover** account yet, create one by downloading the app on your mobile device.

Then, add the channel inside IFTTT:

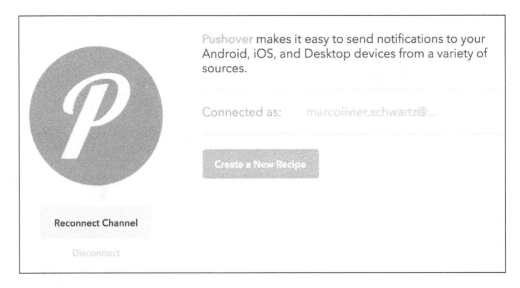

Pushover makes it easy to send notifications to your Android, iOS, and Desktop devices from a variety of sources.

Connected as: marcolivier.schwartz@...

Create a New Recipe

Reconnect Channel

Disconnect

Next, we are going to need some sensors connected to your Arduino board. Please see the previous chapter to see how to connect a photocell and the **DHT11** sensor to your Arduino board.

How to do it...

We are now going to create our first IFTTT recipe:

1. Create a new recipe, and select the **Maker** channel as the trigger:

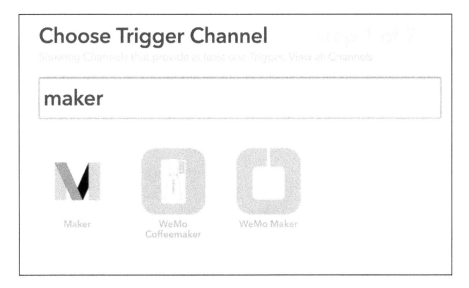

2. Name the event `alert`:

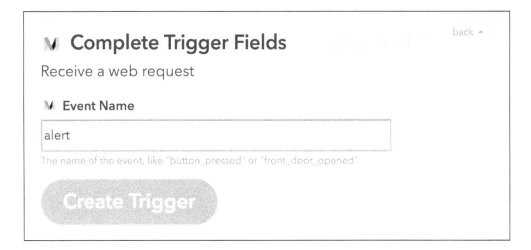

3. Next, select `Pushover` as the **action channel**:

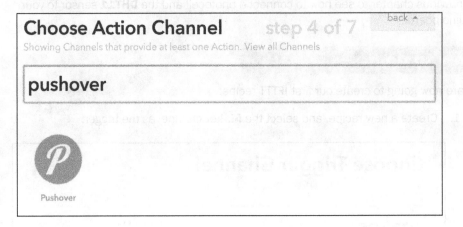

4. As for the notification, we'll simply name it `Alert`, and write the following message:

5. You can now create the recipe that will appear inside your IFTTT account:

| Maker Event "alert" | Send a Pushover notification |

Let's now write the code for this recipe. As usual, I will only highlight the most important parts of the code here:

1. It starts by including the required libraries:

```
#include <SPI.h>
#include <WiFi101.h>
#include "DHT.h"
```

2. After that, we set the alert that we also set on IFTTT, and also set the IFTTT key:

```
const char* host = "maker.ifttt.com";
const char* eventName   = "alert";
const char* key = "key";
```

3. In the `loop()` function of the sketch, we set a trigger when the humidity reaches more than 30 percent:

```
if (h > 30.00) {
```

4. If that's the case, we prepare a request with the trigger name we defined earlier, along with the **Maker** channel key:

```
String url = "/trigger/";
    url += eventName;
    url += "/with/key/";
    url += key;
```

5. If that's the case, we send a request to the IFTTT server:

```
client.print(String("GET ") + url + " HTTP/1.1\r\n" +
                "Host: " + host + "\r\n" +
                "Connection: close\r\n\r\n");
```

```
    int timeout = millis() + 5000;
    while (client.available() == 0) {
      if (timeout - millis() < 0) {
        Serial.println(">>> Client Timeout !");
        client.stop();
        return;
      }
    }
```

6. It's now time to test the project! Grab the code from the GitHub repository of this book, and then make sure to modify it with your WiFi credentials, and IFTTT Maker key. Then, upload the code to the board.

If the humidity then crosses the threshold, you should quickly receive an alert on your phone:

How it works...

This recipe really showcased the power of IFTTT: by creating recipes on IFTTT, you can easily trigger events from your Arduino board, and have IFTTT do a given action for you as a response.

See also

In the next recipe, we are going to see how to send email notifications from IFTTT.

Sending text message notifications

In this recipe, we'll continue using IFTTT, but this time we are going to see how to send data along with the trigger coming from the board. This will allow us to actually send data via IFTTT. To illustrate this, we'll send data right on your phone via text messages.

Getting ready

For this recipe, you will need to have your board connected to sensors just like in the previous recipe. You will also need to connect the SMS channel to your IFTTT account:

1. Create a new recipe, and name the event `text_data`:

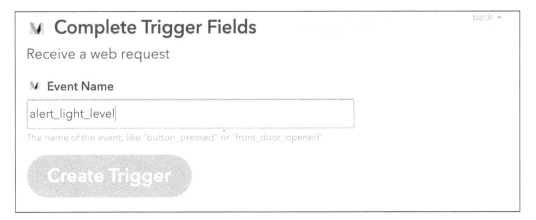

2. After that, select SMS as the **action channel**:

3. This time, we are actually going to send data with the request, and this data is available as `Value1`, `Value2`, and so on. Therefore, this is the message we are going to use:

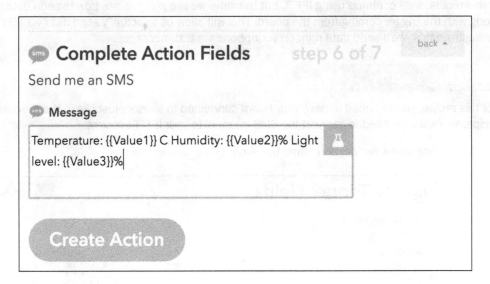

4. This is how the final recipe should look like:

How to do it...

Now, let's see how to configure the Arduino board. As the code is very similar to the one from the last recipe, I will only highlight the changes here.

Same as before, you need to enter your IFTTT key:

```
const char* host = "maker.ifttt.com";
const char* eventName  = "text_data";
const char* key = "key";
```

For the request, we actually need to pass the different measurements done by the board, so the temperature, humidity, and light level:

```
String url = "/trigger/";
  url += eventName;
  url += "/with/key/";
  url += key;
  url += "?value1=";
  url += String(t);
  url += "&value2=";
  url += String(h);
  url += "&value3=";
  url += String(lightLevel);
```

You can now grab the code from the GitHub repository of this book, and make sure to modify the code with your credentials. Then, upload the code to your board.

You should quickly receive an SMS similar to this:

To: SMS

SMS with SMS
Today 09:50

Temperature: 26.00 C Humidity: 33.00% Light level: 89.06%

Note that there is currently a 100 SMS per month limit for users in the US and Canada, and 10 per month outside. Make sure to tune your project accordingly so it doesn't reach this limit.

How it works...

In this recipe, we pushed things further with IFTTT and learned how to actually transmit data via the Maker channel, so you can use it inside your IFTTT actions as well.

See also

I now advice you to follow the last recipe of this chapter to learn how to actually log this data into an online spreadsheet.

Storing data on Google Drive

In this last recipe of this chapter, we are going to see how to use our Arduino board and IFTTT to log measured data right on a Google Drive spreadsheet, so it can be accessed from anywhere in the world.

Getting ready

Before building this recipe, we need to connect the Google Drive channel to your account:

1. You will simply need to log in to your Google account from IFTTT, authorize the app, and then you'll be able to see the Google Drive channel inside your IFTTT account:

Google Drive lets you store and access your files anywhere – on the web, on your hard drive, or on the go.

Email address: marcolivier.schwartz@gmail.com

Create a New Recipe

⚙ Google Drive Settings

🔒 Google Permissions

Reconnect Channel

Disconnect

2. Now, create a new recipe, use the **Maker** channel as the trigger, and name the event `google_data`:

3. As the **action channel**, choose **Google Drive**, and then select the **Add row to spreadsheet** action:

4. Next, leave it as it is for the row to be appended to the spreadsheet, as it already contains all the data that we want to log:

5. Finally, create the recipe, and check that it is activated.

How to do it...

We are now going to configure our Arduino board for this project. Again, as it is really similar to the last recipe we saw in this chapter, I will only highlight the main differences here.

You need to set your IFTTT **Maker** key inside the code:

```
const char* host = "maker.ifttt.com";
const char* eventName   = "google_data";
const char* key = "key";
```

The rest of the code is strictly the same as for the previous recipe, as we are transmitting the same data.

Now, grab the code from the GitHub repository of this book, modify it with your own WiFi network credentials and IFTTT Maker key, and upload the code to the board.

Then, go to your Google Drive account. You should quickly see that a new file was created, called `IFTTT_Maker_Events`. Open this file and you should see that the first row was added to the sheet:

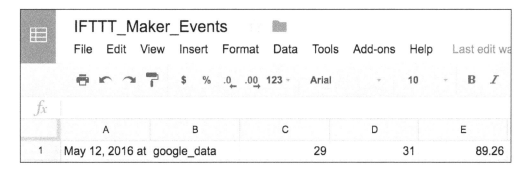

After a while, more data will be logged inside the sheet:

	A	B	C	D	E
1	**Date**	**Event**	**Temperature**	**Humidity**	**Light Level**
2	May 12, 2016 at 07:53PM	google_data	29	31	89.26
3	May 12, 2016 at 07:54PM	google_data	26	33	88.96
4	May 12, 2016 at 07:55PM	google_data	26	33	88.96

You can now also use the plotting functions of Google Spreadsheets to plot the data as it comes into the spreadsheet. For example, I plotted all the light level measurements into a single graph:

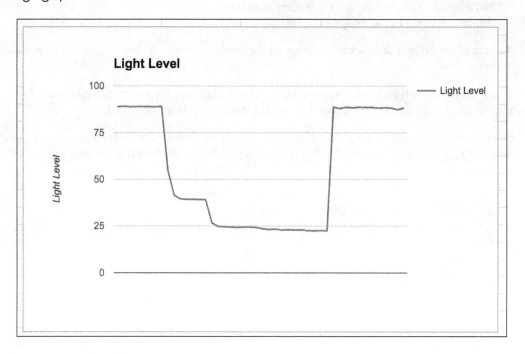

How it works...

Just like the other recipes of this chapter, we interacted with Google Drive from your Arduino board, using IFTTT as an intermediary. This allowed us to easily log measurement data inside Google Drive.

See also

As this is the last recipe of this chapter, I now recommend checking the next section in case you had any issues.

Troubleshooting issues with web services

In this part of the chapter, we are going to see what can go wrong when using your Arduino board to interact with web services. Indeed, some of the steps involved here are quite complex and many things can go differently than expected.

Updates

The first thing that can happen is incorrectly entering your Twitter API keys or Facebook access token inside the Arduino sketch. Also make sure that you correctly entered the callback URL inside the Facebook app settings. Finally, make sure that you didn't reach the calls limit on Temboo.

No notifications are triggered

If you don't receive any notifications from IFTTT, either via push notifications or text messages, first check that you entered the correct Maker key for IFTTT inside the sketch, as well as the correct event name. Also check that the recipe is still marked as active on IFTTT. Finally, make sure that you are connected to the Internet with your Arduino board, and that the sensors connected to the board are working correctly.

Machine-to-Machine Interactions

4

In this chapter, we will cover:

- ▸ Types of IoT interaction
- ▸ Basic local M2M interactions
- ▸ Cloud M2M with IFTTT
- ▸ M2M alarm system
- ▸ Automated light controller
- ▸ Automated sprinkler controller
- ▸ Troubleshooting basic M2M issues

Introduction

In the previous chapters of this book, we learned how to interact with the Arduino board via the Web, either to visualize measurements made by the board, or to automatically interact with web services.

In this chapter, we are actually going to focus on something different: making two (or more) Arduino boards talk to each other and interact with each other, without any human intervention. This is known as Machine-to-Machine communications, and is a very exciting field of the IoT. Let's dive in!

Types of IoT interaction

There are many possible interactions between devices and users in the world of the Internet of Things, and before we start this chapter I want to give you an overview of all the possible scenarios.

The one we have already seen in this book is machine-human interaction, where we use an IoT device to log data on a server, which is then used to display a graph that can be understood and used by the final user.

The second type of interaction is human-machine interaction, where the user is triggering a command to a remote device, for example, to activate a lamp remotely.

Finally, the last scenario is machine-to-machine interaction, where two or more devices are directly talking to each other, without the intervention of any human. This is the type of interaction that we are going to focus on in this chapter.

See also

I now recommend checking the next recipe in this chapter, to begin to have an understanding of what a **Machine-to-Machine** (**M2M**) interaction looks like between Arduino devices.

Basic local M2M interactions

In the first project of this chapter, we are going to learn how to make a very simple case of Machine-to-Machine interaction, by using two Arduino MKR1000 boards. To illustrate M2M communications, we are just going to make them talk via the local Wi-Fi network.

Getting ready

This project will be composed of two Arduino boards. One board will be connected to a simple push button, and the other one to a simple LED. The goal is that whenever the button is pressed, the first board will send the signal to the other board to light up the LED.

These are the components that we will need for this recipe:

- Arduino MKR1000 board x2 (https://www.adafruit.com/products/3156)
- Push button (https://www.sparkfun.com/products/97)
- 1K Ohmresistor (https://www.sparkfun.com/products/13760)
- LED (https://www.sparkfun.com/products/9590)
- 330Ohm resistor (https://www.sparkfun.com/products/8377)

Let's now see how to assemble the board with the push button. The first step is to place the push button on the breadboard, along with the resistor, connected to one pin of the push button. Then, also connect the pin of the push button to pin 6 of the Arduino board. Finally, connect the other side of the push button to the VCC pin of the Arduino board.

This is the final result:

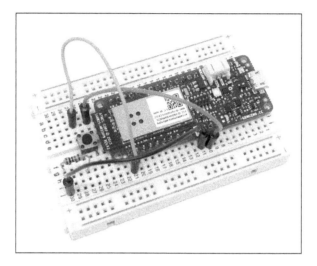

Let's now assemble the other board, with the LED. For this one, first place the LED in series with the resistor on the board, with the longest pin of the LED connected to the resistor. Then, connect the other pin of the resistor to pin 6 on the Arduino board, and the other part of the LED to GND.

This is the final result:

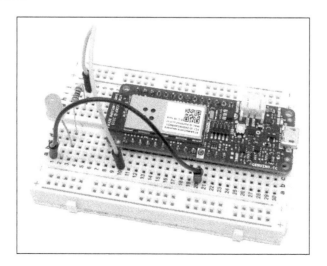

On the software side, you will also need the REST library for Arduino that you can install from the Arduino library manager.

How to do it...

We are now going to see how to configure the boards, starting with the board you assembled last – the LED board. As usual, I will only highlight the most important parts of the code here, and you will find the complete code on the GitHub repository of this book:

1. The sketch starts by importing the required libraries:

    ```
    #include <SPI.h>
    #include <WiFi101.h>
    #include <aREST.h>
    ```

2. Then, we declare the aREST object, which we will use to receive commands from the other Arduino board:

    ```
    aREST rest = aREST();
    ```

3. We also declare the pin connected to the LED as the output:

    ```
    pinMode(6, OUTPUT);
    ```

4. Now, grab the whole code for this project from the GitHub repository of this book from `https://github.com/marcoschwartz/iot-arduino-cookbook`.

5. After that, modify the code with your Wi-Fi credentials, and upload the code to the board. Then, open the Serial monitor. Check what the IP address of the board is – you will need it soon.

6. Let's now configure the board with the push button. It also starts by importing the right libraries:

    ```
    #include <SPI.h>
    #include <WiFi101.h>
    ```

7. Then, you need to enter the IP address of the LED board:

    ```
    const char* host = "192.168.0.108";
    ```

8. Then, we constantly check if the button was pressed:

    ```
    if (digitalRead(6)) {
    ```

9. If so, we call a function on the LED board that will toggle the state of the LED:

    ```
    String url = "/toggle";

      Serial.print("Requesting URL: ");
      Serial.println(url);
    ```

```
// This will send the request to the server
client.print(String("GET ") + url + " HTTP/1.1\r\n" +
             "Host: " + host + "\r\n" +
             "Connection: close\r\n\r\n");
unsigned long timeout = millis();
while (client.available() == 0) {
  if (millis() - timeout > 5000) {
    Serial.println(">>> Client Timeout !");
    client.stop();
    return;
  }
}
```

10. You can now grab the code for this board from the GitHub repository of this book again, and upload it to the board.

11. You can now finally test the project. Press the button on one board, and it should immediately toggle the state of the LED on the other board.

How it works...

This recipe illustrated how two boards can communicate with each other, with the first board sending a message to the other one when a given event is triggered (here, the press of a button).

See also

I now suggest reading the next recipe, where you will learn how to do the exact same project, but this time by having both boards communicate in the cloud.

Cloud M2M with IFTTT

In the previous recipe, we saw a good example of how to make two Arduino boards talk within your own local Wi-Fi network. However, it was not convenient, for example, you had to enter the IP address of one device in the sketch of the other device.

In this recipe, we are going to use IFTTT again (that we already used in the previous chapter) to make the devices talk, but this time via the Internet. We'll see that it greatly simplifies everything, and that it, of course, allows the devices to be anywhere in the world.

Getting ready

First, make sure that you have two boards assembled just as in the previous recipe. You will also need an account at IFTTT, with the **Maker** channel connected.

You will also need to install the `PubSubClient` library that you can find inside the Arduino library manager.

I'll now show you what you need to modify on each board to make the boards talk via IFTTT. Of course, you will find the complete code inside the GitHub repository of this book.

In this recipe, the first board (with the push button) will actually send a trigger to IFTTT, which in response will send a command to the `aREST.io` cloud server. This server will then relay the command to the other board, toggling the state of the LED. I will, of course, show you how to connect the second board to `aREST.io`, so it can be controlled from anywhere.

For the board connected to the push button, you need to add information about IFTTT, including your **Maker** channel key:

```
const char* host = "maker.ifttt.com";
const char* eventName   = "toggle";
const char* key = "key";
```

Then, the request needs to be modified with the correct trigger and the key:

```
String url = "/trigger/";
  url += eventName;
  url += "/with/key/";
  url += key;
```

For the other board, you need to include all the required libraries:

```
#include <SPI.h>
#include <WiFi101.h>
#include <PubSubClient.h>
#include <aREST.h>
```

Next, we define a `WiFiClient` and `PubSubClient`:

```
WiFiClient wifiClient;
PubSubClient client(wifiClient);
```

We then pass this client to the `aREST` instance:

```
aREST rest = aREST(client);
```

Next, we create a variable that will hold the current state of the LED:

```
bool ledState = false;
```

Just as in the previous recipe, we create a function to toggle the state of the LED:

```
int ledToggle(String command);
```

Inside the `setup()` function, we set an ID to the board:

```
rest.set_id("305eyf");
```

You need to change this, as it will identify your device on the aREST cloud server.

We also expose this function to the aREST API, so it can be called remotely:

```
rest.function("toggle", ledToggle);
```

Finally, here is the detail of the function to toggle the state of the LED:

```
int ledToggle(String command) {

  ledState = !ledState;

  digitalWrite(6, ledState);
  return 1;
}
```

You can now grab both sketches from the GitHub repository of the book, modify them with your own Wi-Fi and IFTTT credentials, and configure both boards.

How to do it...

We now still need to do the link between both boards, via IFTTT. Simply log into your IFTTT account, and create a new recipe. As the trigger channel, choose the **Maker** channel:

Then, type `toggle` as the event, the same as inside the sketch:

As the **action channel**, again select the **Maker** channel:

Now, enter the following command inside the action fields, of course by changing the ID of your board to the one you set inside the sketch:

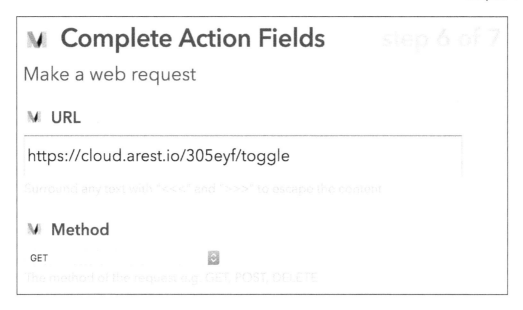

Once the recipe is created, you can immediately try the sketch again. Whenever you press the button, the LED should switch its state. Note that here there might be a 1-2 second delay, because the information needs to go through the IFTTT servers first.

How it works...

This recipe achieves the exact same functionality as the last one. However, here, both boards are truly communication via the cloud, using the IFTTT service. This way, they could actually be anywhere in the world, and the project would still work just as well.

See also

I now recommend checking the next recipe that will teach you how to actually build a project with M2M communications: a cloud alarm system.

M2M alarm system

In this recipe, we are going to apply what we have learned so far about M2M communications to build a simple alarm system that will be completely based on cloud M2M interactions. There will be one or many motion sensors that will send alarm triggers to a central station composed of an LED and a small buzzer.

Getting ready

There are two parts in this project: the motion sensor module, and the central base module with an LED and a sound buzzer.

This is the list of the required components for this recipe, not counting the Arduino MKR1000 boards and the breadboards and wires:

- ▸ PIR motion sensor (`https://www.sparkfun.com/products/13285`)
- ▸ LED (`https://www.sparkfun.com/products/9590`)
- ▸ 330 Ohm resistor (`https://www.sparkfun.com/products/8377`)
- ▸ Small buzzer (`https://www.adafruit.com/products/160`)

Let's now see how to assemble those modules. We are going to start with the motion sensor module. Simply connect the VCC pin of the PIR motion to the VCC of the Arduino board, GND to GND, and finally the OUT pin of the sensor to pin 6 of the Arduino board.

This is the final result:

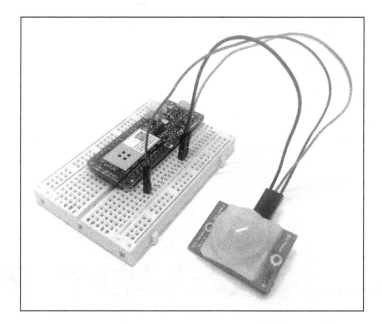

Of course, you can use as many of those modules as you want in this project – they will also work seamlessly with the software we'll set in place.

Let's now see how to assemble the central alarm station. First, place the LED in series with the resistor on the breadboard, as well as the small sound buzzer.

Then, connect the other end of the LED to GND, and the other end of the resistor to GND. For the buzzer, connect one end of the buzzer (marked with a **+**) to Arduino pin **6**, and the other end to GND.

This is the final result:

How to do it...

We are now going to configure the boards we just assembled, starting with the one with the motion sensor. This module will automatically send an alert to IFTTT in case motion is detected.

Actually, it is very similar to the sketch for the board with the push button in the previous recipe, you just need to change the event name:

```
const char* host = "maker.ifttt.com";
const char* eventName   = "alarm";
const char* key = "key";
```

For the other module, we are still going to use the aREST framework to connect the board to the cloud. We need to define a function called `activateAlarm`:

```
int activateAlarm(String command);
```

Here are the details of this function:

```
int activateAlarm(String command) {
```

```
    tone(7, 500);
    digitalWrite(6, HIGH);

    return 1;
}
```

It basically activates the buzzer, and also turns the LED on. We will call this function whenever a motion sensor senses motion nearby.

You can now grab all the code for both modules from the GitHub repository of the book, change the credentials inside the sketches, and upload the code to the boards.

Next, log into your IFTTT account, and create a new recipe. As the trigger channel, choose the **Maker** channel, with the following event:

For the action channel, again choose the **Maker** channel, with the **Make a web request** action:

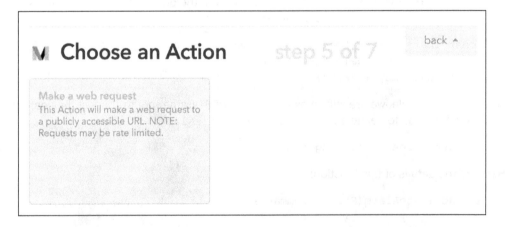

For the action itself, again enter the ID of the target device, along with the alarm function:

This will make sure that the `aREST.io` server is called whenever an alert is received from any of the motion sensors.

You can now complete the creation of the recipe, and actually try the project. Try to pass your hand in front of the motion sensor – you should nearly immediately see the LED of the base station turning on, and you should also hear a loud sound coming from the buzzer!

How it works...

This alarm system works completely in the cloud, with boards talking to each other via IFTTT. This is a great example of an M2M system, where several boards are exchanging information with each other.

> The nice thing here is that there is also no additional code to set to add more motion sensors – just configure them with the same sketch, and they will all immediately work within the recipe we created on IFTTT.

See also

I now suggest you check out the following two recipes, to discover more M2M projects with the Arduino MKR1000 board.

Automated light controller

Inside this recipe, we are going to continue exploring M2M communications with the Arduino MKR1000 board, this time by creating an automated light controller based on Arduino. A first module will be in charge of detecting the ambient light level, and then sending alerts to a second module, which will switch a light on or off, depending on the received alert.

Getting ready

To control a lamp in this project, we are going to use a very convenient component called the PowerSwitch Tail:

These components allow us to easily control devices powered by the mains electricity from an Arduino board, as you can just plug it into the mains electricity and then plug your device into it as well.

This is the list of the components that will be required for this recipe:

▶ PowerSwitch Tail (https://www.adafruit.com/products/268)

▶ Photocell (https://www.sparkfun.com/products/9088)

▶ 10K Ohm resistor (https://www.sparkfun.com/products/8374)

Let's now assemble the hardware for this recipe. We are going to start with the module connected to the lamp. Simply plug the GND and Vin- pins to the GND on the Arduino board, and the Vin+ to pin 6 of the Arduino board.

This is the final result:

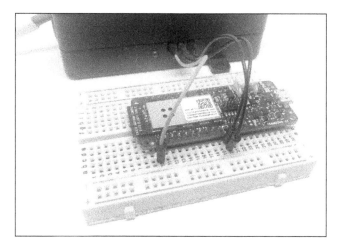

Also don't forget to plug a device into the PowerSwitch, and also connect it to the mains electricity. In this example, I used a simple 30W desk lamp.

Let's now assemble the board that will be connected to the photocell. Simply place the photocell in series with the resistor on the board, and then connect the common pin-to-pin A0 of the board. Then, connect the other end of the resistor to GND, and the other end of the photocell to VCC.

This is the final result:

How to do it...

Let's now see how to configure these boards. We are going to start with the board connected to the photocell.

Inside the code, we need to define two thresholds: one when it's too dark, and one when it's bright enough:

```
int light_threshold_low = 30;
int light_threshold_high = 50;
```

Of course, feel free to change these as you see fit. Then, in the `loop()` function of the sketch, we need to measure the current value from the photocell, calculated in percent:

```
int sensorValue = analogRead(sensorPin);
float lightLevel = sensorValue/1024.*100;
```

We then test this value to see if it's above the high threshold:

```
if (lightLevel > light_threshold_high) {
```

If so, we send the following alert to IFTTT:

```
String url = "/trigger/light_high";
  url += "/with/key/";
  url += key;
```

We, of course, do a similar action if the light level is below the low level.

For the module connected to the lamp, things are easier. It's basically the exact same sketch as we saw for the alarm base station in the previous recipe. Here, you just need to set pin 6 as an output:

```
pinMode(6, OUTPUT);
```

You can now grab all the code from the GitHub repository of the book, modify the sketches with your own credentials, and upload the code to the boards.

Then, go to IFTTT, and start the creation of a first recipe. As the trigger channel, choose the **Maker** channel with the `light_low` event:

As for the action, again choose the **Maker** channel, sending the command to set pin 6 on a high state:

 Of course, you'll need to make sure to modify the ID of the device with the one you set inside the sketch.

Then, create another recipe, with the same channels, but this time with the `light_high` event:

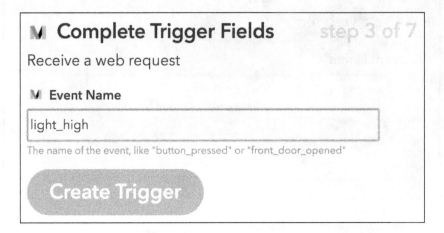

For the action, it's the same as before, but this time we set pin 6 to a LOW state:

Once you have confirmed the creation of this recipe, you can test the project. Try, for example, to hide the photocell with your hands: the lamp should automatically turn on after a few seconds.

How it works...

In this project, we again have two devices that communicate with each other via IFTTT. Together, they form an autonomous lamp controller system, where no human intervention is needed.

Note that as the devices are communicating via IFTTT, they would work perfectly in different Wi-Fi networks.

See also

I now recommend checking the last recipe of the chapter, where you will learn how to build an automated sprinkler controller.

Automated sprinkler controller

For the last recipe of the chapter, we are going to see how to make a cool project to automate your garden: an automated sprinkler controller that also works via the cloud. We'll have two Arduino boards communicating with each other: a first board to measure the soil moisture, and a second one to control a pump to water the plants or anything else in your garden.

Getting ready

The project will be composed of two parts again. The first part will simply be an Arduino MKR1000 board, along with a moisture sensor based on the SHT10 sensor. The second part of the project will be a simple Arduino board as well, connected to a relay. The relay can then be used to control a little pump or sprinkler that you already have.

This is the list of components that are required for this recipe:

- Soil moisture sensor (https://www.adafruit.com/products/1298)
- Relay (https://www.pololu.com/product/2480)
- 10K Ohm resistor (https://www.sparkfun.com/products/8374)

Let's now assemble the project, starting with connecting the Arduino board to the sensor. First, connect the sensor to the breadboard, and then place the 10K Ohm resistor between the data and the VCC pins of the sensor (the blue and red wires).

Then, connect the black or green wire to GND, the red wire to VCC, the yellow cable to pin 6 of the Arduino board, and the blue wire to pin 7.

This is the final result:

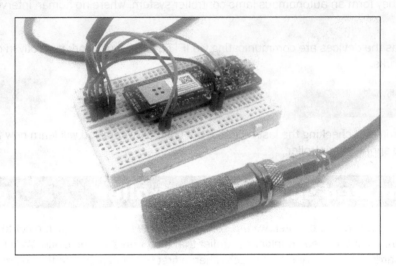

For the relay board, things are easier. Just connect the relay VCC pin to VCC, the GND pin to GND, and finally the SIG pin to Arduino pin 6.

This is the final result:

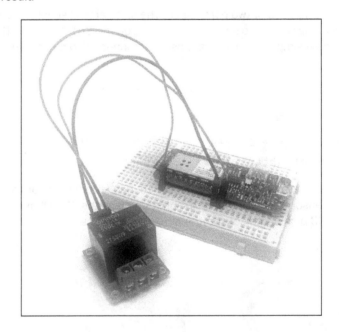

You will also need to install the SHT1x library that you can find at `https://github.com/practicalarduino/SHT1x`.

Now, let's first test the board with the moisture sensor, to make sure the connections were made correctly. It starts by including the sensor's library:

```
#include <SHT1x.h>
```

Next, define the pins to which the sensor is connected, and create an instance of the sensor:

```
#define dataPin   6
#define clockPin 7
SHT1x sht1x(dataPin, clockPin);
```

After that, inside the `loop()` function of the sketch, we perform the measurements on the sensor:

```
float temp_c;
  float temp_f;
  float humidity;

  // Read values from the sensor
  temp_c = sht1x.readTemperatureC();
  temp_f = sht1x.readTemperatureF();
  humidity = sht1x.readHumidity();
```

Finally, we print these measurements and repeat the operation every two seconds:

```
Serial.print("Temperature: ");
  Serial.print(temp_c, DEC);
  Serial.print("C / ");
  Serial.print(temp_f, DEC);
  Serial.print("F. Humidity: ");
  Serial.print(humidity);
  Serial.println("%");

  delay(2000);
```

You can now grab the code from the GitHub repository of the book, and upload it to the board. Then, open the Serial monitor. This is what you should see:

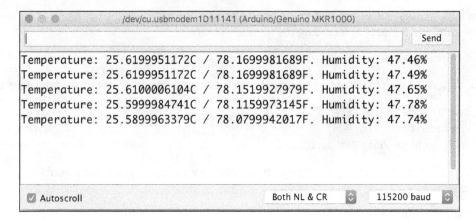

If you can see numbers that make sense, congratulations! Your soil moisture sensor is correctly wired to the Arduino board.

How to do it...

We are now going to configure both boards, so they can communicate via IFTTT. Inside the sketch for the board connected to the soil moisture sensor, you need to set two thresholds:

```
float humidity_threshold_low = 20;
float humidity_threshold_high = 40;
```

Basically, the lowest threshold is the one at which we'll start to water the plants. When the soil moisture reaches the highest threshold, we'll stop the pump or sprinkler again.

Then, in the loop() function of the sketch, we will test to see if the humidity is high:

```
if (humidity > humidity_threshold_high) {
```

If so, we send the corresponding alert to IFTTT:

```
String url = "/trigger/humidity_high";
  url += "/with/key/";
  url += key;
```

We also check if the humidity is low:

```
if (humidity < humidity_threshold_low) {
```

If so, we send the relevant trigger to IFTTT:

```
String url = "/trigger/humidity_low";
  url += "/with/key/";
  url += key;
```

The sketch for the board connected to the relay is strictly the same as the lamp controller in the previous sketch. You will, of course, find it inside the GitHub repository of the book as well.

You can now grab the complete code from the GitHub repository of the book, modify the sketches with your own credentials, and then upload the code to the boards.

Next, go to IFTTT again, and create a new recipe. For the trigger channel, again choose the **Maker** channel, with the following event name:

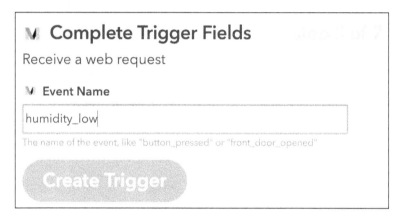

For the action, choose the **Maker** channel, and enter the following URL (changing the device ID to the one you set inside the sketch):

Indeed, if the humidity gets low, we want to activate the pump. Now, also create a similar recipe to handle the case where the humidity gets too high and we want to stop the pump.

You can now test the project! If you want to test it in real conditions, you can, for example, use a simple plant in a pot, and put the soil moisture sensor in it. This is how I tested the project:

If the humidity is too low, it should automatically activate the relay on the second board. You can now connect the relay to the pump or sprinkler system of your choice.

How it works...

This projects works by making two boards communicate via IFTTT, this time to create a project that you can actually use in your garden or your home for your plants.

See also

As this was the last recipe in the book, I suggest checking the last section of this chapter in case you had issues with the recipes in this chapter.

Troubleshooting basic M2M issues

In this part of the chapter, we are going to see what can go wrong when building M2M projects using Arduino.

Pushing the button doesn't do anything

The first thing that can happen is that the button is not correctly wired to the Arduino board. Make sure that you followed the wiring instructions. You can also check the lights on the Arduino board when you press the button: a light should turn on whenever the board is sending data, so this is what you should see when pressing the button.

The pump/sprinkler doesn't get activated

One simple reason for this problem is that the humidity doesn't get low enough for the board to send an alert. What I recommend doing is checking the humidity level with the test sketch of the sensor. If needed, adjust the thresholds inside the code to make the board send correct alerts depending on the level of humidity you want for your plants `http://www.kasetophono.com/2014/10/night.html`.

Home Automation Projects

5

In this chapter, we will cover:

- Controlling your coffee machine from the cloud
- Dim LEDs from anywhere in the world
- Remote controlled garage door
- Controlling the access to your door remotely
- Cloud smoke detector
- Smart cloud thermostat
- Home automation dashboard in the cloud
- Troubleshooting home automation project issues

Introduction

In this chapter, we are going to see how to apply what we have learned so far in this book to the home automation field. We are going to use the Arduino board to build several home automation projects that will all be accessible from anywhere in the world and communicating with cloud services.

We are, for example, going to see how to control a coffee machine, how to open your garage door remotely, and how to detect smoke in your home and be alerted immediately. At the end of this chapter, we are going to see how to combine several of those projects, for example, to build a cloud thermostat.

Controlling your coffee machine from the cloud

In this first recipe of this chapter, we are going to learn how to control a coffee machine from anywhere in the world. Of course, it could be any other appliance, such as a lamp or an oven. We are going to see how to connect the coffee machine to the Arduino MKR1000 board, and then how to connect the board to a cloud dashboard so it can easily be controlled remotely.

Getting ready

Let's first see how to connect the Arduino board to the coffee machine, or to any home appliance.

To do that, we are going to use a component called the PowerSwitch Tail, which can be used to control any appliance with Arduino. You can get this component from http://www.powerswitchtail.com/Pages/default.aspx.

You could, of course, also use a simple relay, but using the PowerSwitch Tail is much safer to connect electrical devices.

To connect the PowerSwitch Tail to Arduino, simply start by connecting the Vin+ pin of the PowerSwitch to Arduino pin 6, and then the two remaining pins to the GND pin of the Arduino board.

Then, connect the appliance you want to control to the female plug on the PowerSwitch, and then the male plug to the mains electricity.

This is an image of the final result:

On the software side, and for the rest of this chapter, we are going to use two Arduino libraries: the `aREST` library, and the `PubSubClient` library. This will allow us to control our Arduino board from anywhere in the world. You can install them both from the Arduino library manager.

How to do it...

Let's now see how to configure the board so it can be controlled remotely. As usual, I will only highlight the main features of the code here, as this is similar to what we already saw in the previous chapter. We first need to include the required libraries:

```
#include <SPI.h>
#include <WiFi101.h>
#include <PubSubClient.h>
#include <aREST.h>
```

Then, we also need to set the Wi-Fi name and password of the board:

```
const char* ssid     = "wifi-name";
const char* password = "wifi-password";
```

Inside the `setup()` function, we give an ID and a name to the device:

```
rest.set_id("362c3s");
rest.set_name("coffee");
```

Finally, we also need to set pin number 6 as an output:

```
pinMode(6, OUTPUT);
```

Now, simply grab the whole code from the GitHub repository of this book, and make sure to modify it with your own Wi-Fi credentials and device ID. Then, upload the code to the board.

The next step is to create an account at `http://dashboard.arest.io/`.

You will then be able to create a new dashboard:

Inside the dashboard, create a new element by entering the ID of the device, and also by choosing a `digital` command on pin 6. This should be the result:

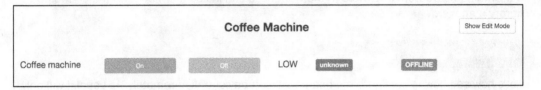

You can now try it already: just press the **On** button, and the appliance should turn on immediately. Of course, you have to turn it **On** the appliance itself, for example, turn the power switch to **On** on a **Coffee machine**.

How it works...

The project works by first connecting the Arduino board to the `aREST.io` cloud server, and then by controlling the board (and therefore the appliance) using a cloud dashboard. Therefore, the appliance is now available from anywhere in the world.

There's more...

You can also build other projects based on this one. For example, you could use IFTTT to automatically turn on your coffee machine every morning at a given time, to lose no time at breakfast.

See also

I now recommend checking the next project to learn more about how to build more cloud-connected home automation projects with the Arduino MKR1000 board.

Dim LEDs from anywhere in the world

You have probably already seen those LED strips that you can control remotely. We are going to do the same in this recipe (with three LEDs of different colors), but in this project you'll be able to control those LEDs from anywhere in the world.

Getting ready

For this recipe, you are going to need three LEDs of different colors (I used a blue one, a red one, and a green one). For each of those LEDs, you will also need a 330 Ohm resistor.

To assemble the project, first place all the LEDs on the breadboard, with each one of them connected in series with a resistor, the longest pin of each LED connected to the resistors. Then, connect all the free pins of the LEDs to the GND pin of the Arduino board. Finally, connect free pins of the resistors to Arduino pins 3, 4, and 5.

This is the final result:

How to do it...

We are now going to configure the board. As the sketch is nearly the same as the previous recipe, I will only highlight the main differences here.

Inside the `setup()` function of the sketch, we need to set an ID for the device, as well as a name:

```
rest.set_id("305eyf");
rest.set_name("led_dimmer");
```

Now, simply grab the whole code from the GitHub repository of this book, and make sure to modify it with your own Wi-Fi credentials and device ID. Then, upload the code to the board.

Again, go to the same aREST cloud dashboard website that we used in the previous recipe, and create a new dashboard for our LEDs:

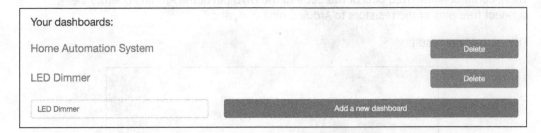

For each LED, create an element inside the dashboard with the following parameters:

Of course, you might have connected the LEDs to different pins than me, so make sure you are correctly naming each element with the right color. This should be the final result:

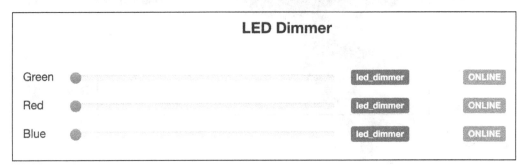

You can now finally try the project! Try to change the value of the sliders by dragging the cursor:

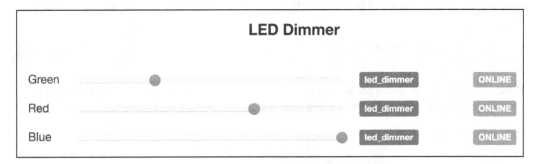

You should immediately see the result on the project:

Congratulations, you can now dim and control LEDs from anywhere in the world!

How it works...

The project works again by connecting the board to a cloud server, which then receives commands via a cloud dashboard. Moving the sliders on the dashboard has the same effect as an `analogWrite()` function on the Arduino board, therefore allowing us to dim the LEDs on command.

There's more...

Again, it would be easy to combine this project with IFTTT, for example, to automatically dim the LEDs as the night falls. You could also use LED strips instead of individual LEDs, the approach would be exactly the same.

See also

I now recommend checking the next recipes of this chapter for more home automation projects!

Remote controlled garage door

In this recipe, we are going to build a very useful project to automate your home: a garage door controller. Not only will you be able to control the garage door remotely, but you will also automatically receive alerts on your phone whenever the garage door is opened!

Getting ready

All garage doors around the world are different, so in this project I will actually simulate the closing part of a garage door. Then it will be up to you to actually apply it to your own system that you have in your home.

For this recipe, we are going to connect two components to the Arduino board: a relay, which will simulate the garage door motor, and a proximity sensor, which will be used to detect if the garage door is in the closed position.

This is the list of components that we are going to use in this project:

>   Magnetic contact switch (https://www.adafruit.com/products/375)

>   5V Relay (https://www.pololu.com/product/2480)

This is the final result:

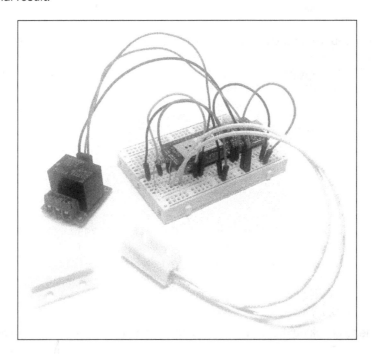

Of course, from there, you will need to actually install the other part of the proximity sensor to the garage door itself, to check that it is opened. However, for this project I'll simply keep it around to simulate the action of having the garage door closed.

How to do it...

Let's now see how to configure this project. We are again going to use IFTTT to send alerts to your phone, so this is something we are already familiar with. You can check the previous chapter again if you need more information about how to use IFTTT:

1. The sketch starts by defining the IFTTT parameters:

```
const char* host = "maker.ifttt.com";
const char* eventName  = "door_closed";
const char* key = "key";
```

2. We also set the ID of the device inside the `setup()` function of the sketch:

```
rest.set_id("305eyf");
rest.set_name("garage_door");
```

3. Then, in the `loop()` function of the sketch, we check if the switch has been activated or not:

```
if (digitalRead(6)) {
```

4. If that's the case, it means the garage door is closed. Then send an alert to IFTTT:

```
String url = "/trigger/";
url += eventName;
url += "/with/key/";
url += key;
```

5. You can now grab the whole code from the GitHub repository of this book, and configure the board with it. Make sure to modify the code to include your Wi-Fi credentials, and also change the code to set your IFTTT Maker key.

6. Then the next step is to go to the dashboard website as in the previous recipes, and create an element to control the relay simulating the garage door:

7. After that, go over to IFTTT and create a new recipe. This recipe will automatically send us an alert when the door is closed. At the trigger channel, choose the **Maker** channel with the following event name:

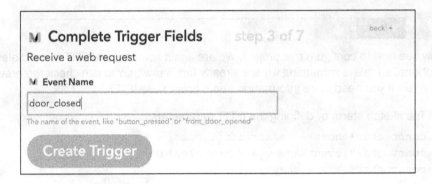

8. As the action channel, choose SMS:

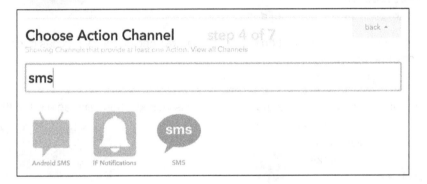

9. I wrote a simple message as the default message that will be sent when the condition is met:

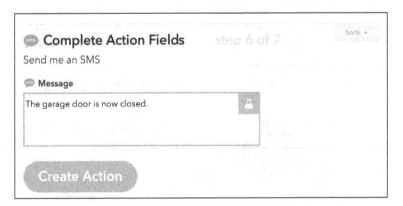

10. It's finally time to test the project! Make sure the board is correctly configured, and try to control the relay from the cloud dashboard. Also, place the other end of the magnetic switch to the one connected to the Arduino board: you should quickly receive a text message informing you that the door was closed:

To: SMS	Details
	SMS with SMS
	Today 08:35
The garage door is now closed.	

How it works...

This project combined aREST (to control the garage door) and IFTTT (to send alerts), showing how easy it is to combine several web services to create complex home automation applications.

There's more...

You can, of course, take everything you learned in this recipe, and apply it to your own garage door. This will require a lot of extra work, but the principles are exactly the same as we saw in this recipe. In no time you'll have a garage door that you can completely control from the cloud and that sends you alerts!

See also

I recommend checking the next recipes in this chapter for even more cloud-connected home automation projects!

Controlling the access to your door remotely

In this recipe, we are going to learn how to open and close a door lock remotely, from anywhere in the world. You will then also be able to share this access with other people, so they too can gain access to this door lock.

Getting ready

For this project, we are going to use an actual electronic door lock that can be controlled from the Arduino board to lock/unlock a door. The component uses 12V as the power supply, so we are going to require an external power supply and some additional components to make it work.

This is the list of required components for this project:

- ▸ Electronic door lock (https://www.adafruit.com/products/1512)
- ▸ 1K Ohm resistor (https://www.sparkfun.com/products/8980)
- ▸ Rectifier diode (https://www.sparkfun.com/products/8589)
- ▸ N-Channel MOSFET (https://www.sparkfun.com/products/10213)
- ▸ DC jack breadboard connector (https://www.sparkfun.com/products/10811)
- ▸ 12V power supply (https://www.sparkfun.com/products/9442)

Let's now see how to assemble the project. As the process is quite complex here, I have created a schematic for you:

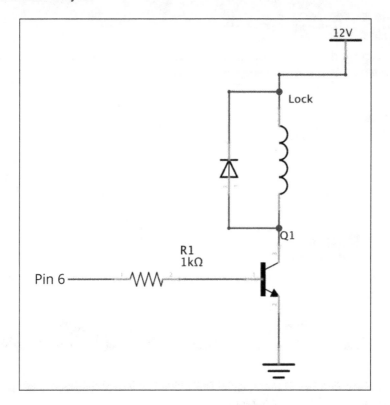

 Make sure to follow the schematic to connect the door lock to the MKR1000 board, via the MOSFET transistor.

This is the final result:

This is a close-up image of the Arduino board:

How to do it...

Let's now see how to configure the board so we can control the door lock remotely. As the sketch is really similar to what we saw earlier in this chapter, I will only highlight the differences here.

You basically just need to assign a unique ID into the code:

```
rest.set_id("305eyf");
rest.set_name("door_lock");
```

Again, go to `http://dashboard.arest.io/`.

You can now create a new dashboard:

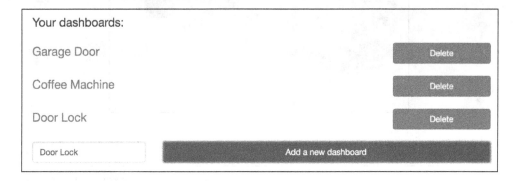

Next, create a new element inside the dashboard, to control the door lock that is connected to Arduino pin 6:

You can now try the project: whenever you click on a button, you should see the door lock reacting instantly, locking or unlocking a door if you mounted the lock on an actual door.

Note that you can also share the door lock with someone by sharing the access to your cloud dashboard, so your friends can use it as well.

How it works...

The project works by connecting the Arduino board to a cloud server. On the board itself, the project uses a power MOSFET to control the door lock that is powered by a 12V power supply.

See also

I now recommend checking the next recipes of this chapter for more exciting home automation projects.

Cloud smoke detector

In several countries around the world, it is not mandatory to install a smoke detector inside your home. In this recipe, we are going to build our own smoke detector that will automatically send you alerts when smoke is detected in your home.

Getting ready

For this recipe, you are going to need a smoke detector, based on the MQ-2 gas sensor. This is the component that I used for this project:

▶ MQ2 smoke sensor (`http://robotbase.en.alibaba.com/ product/1267894712-211851693/MQ2_alcohol_ethanol_gas_sensors. html`)

Let's now see how to assemble this project. First, place the Arduino board on the breadboard. Then, connect the + pin of the sensor to Arduino VCC, the – pin of the sensor to GND, and finally the remaining sensor pin to A0. This is the final result:

We can now test the sensor. Indeed, we need to calibrate it so we know what is the output of the sensor when no smoke is detected. For that, I simply used the default sketch **AnalogReadSerial** given with the Arduino IDE. Upload this sketch to the board, and open the Serial monitor. You should now see the output of the sensor:

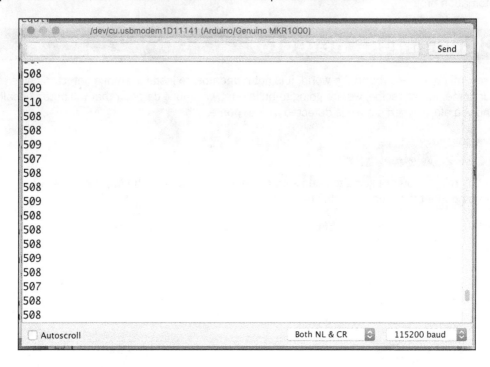

Once this is done, wait for about 20 minutes. Indeed, this is the time the sensor needs to warm up and return a usable signal. After that time, adjust the potentiometer on the sensor's board so the readout value is below 500 (this is the threshold we'll use to detect smoke).

How to do it...

Let's now see how to configure the project so it sends automated alerts to us when smoke is detected. Once again, we are going to use IFTTT to do that, so this is a sketch we have already seen many times in this book. First, we need to set your IFTTT key inside the code, along with the `smoke_detected` event:

```
const char* host = "maker.ifttt.com";
const char* eventName  = "smoke_detected";
const char* key = "key";
```

We also set a trigger to send an event to IFTTT, in case smoke is detected in your home:

```
if (analogRead(A0) > 500) {
```

You can now take the whole code from the GitHub repository of this book, and configure the board with it. Don't forget to enter your Wi-Fi credentials and your IFTTT key inside the code.

Then, go over to IFTTT, and create a new recipe. As the trigger channel, again choose the **Maker** channel, and enter the same event name as in the code:

As the action channel, I chose the SMS channel:

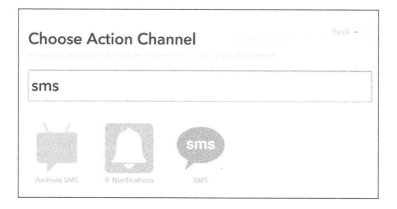

I used a simple alert message:

You can now create the recipe and test it. As for the smoke, I simply placed the sensor in my kitchen when cooking. You can adjust the threshold inside the code or also by playing with the potentiometer, to change the level of smoke detection at which you want to send an alert to your phone.

How it works...

The project is again based on IFTTT, which we use here to send an alert to our phone once a given smoke level is detected by the sensor connected to the Arduino board.

See also

I now recommend checking the last two recipes of this chapter to learn more about how to build more complex home automation systems.

Smart cloud thermostat

In this recipe, we are going to combine several things we have already seen in this chapter, to create a simple thermostat that is completely based on cloud interactions between two Arduino boards.

Getting ready

This project will be based of two different boards: one will measure the temperature and send events to IFTTT, and the other one will be connected to a relay that will simulate an electrical heater.

Let's first see how to assemble the first board. First, place the DHT11 sensor on the breadboard. Then, connect the first pin of the sensor to VCC on the Arduino board, and the last pin of the sensor to the GND pin of the Arduino board. Finally, connect the second pin of the sensor to Arduino pin 6. This is the final result:

For the relay board, simply connect the VCC pin of the relay to Arduino VCC, GND to GND, and finally the SIG pin of the relay to Arduino pin 6. This is the final result:

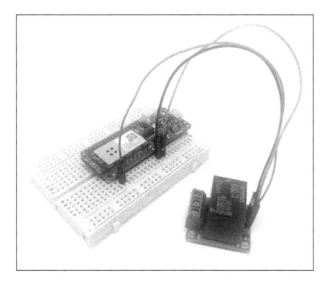

How to do it...

Let's now configure the boards, starting with the one connected to the relay. This sketch is again based on the aREST framework, so it is a sketch that we have already seen several times inside this book.

Inside the sketch, you need to give a unique ID to the relay:

```
rest.set_id("305eyf");
rest.set_name("relay");
```

Then, we also set pin **6** as an output:

```
pinMode(6, OUTPUT);
```

For the other board, the sketch will simply send events to IFTTT, so this will be a sketch that is familiar as well. It starts by including the required libraries:

```
#include <SPI.h>
#include <WiFi101.h>
#include "DHT.h"
```

Then, we define the pin on which the DHT sensor is connected to:

```
#define DHTPIN 6
#define DHTTYPE DHT11
```

We also create an instance of the DHT sensor:

```
DHT dht(DHTPIN, DHTTYPE, 15);
```

Then, we set a target temperature, which is the value that the thermostat will always try to reach:

```
float temperature_target = 25;
```

Inside the `loop()` function of the sketch, we constantly measure the temperature, and check if we are going above or below the threshold. For example, this line tests if we are above the threshold by one degree:

```
if (temperature > temperature_target + 1) {
```

If that's the case, we send the corresponding event to IFTTT:

```
String url = "/trigger/temperature_high";
url += "/with/key/";
url += key;
```

We of course do exactly the same if the temperature gets too low.

You can now grab the whole code from the GitHub repository of this book, modify the code with your credentials (Wi-Fi and IFTTT), and upload the code to the respective boards.

Then, go over to IFTTT, and create a new recipe with the following event as the trigger in the **Maker** channel:

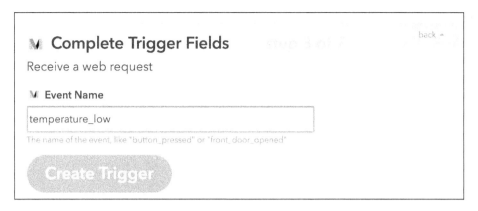

As a result of the temperature being too low, we need to turn on the heater, here the relay. For that, we send the following command to the other board via the `aREST.io` cloud server:

Of course, make sure to modify this command with the ID that you entered in the code. Then, do the same with the `temperature_high` event:

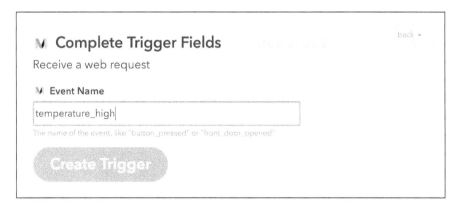

When this trigger is received, we need to turn the heater off again, which is done by this command:

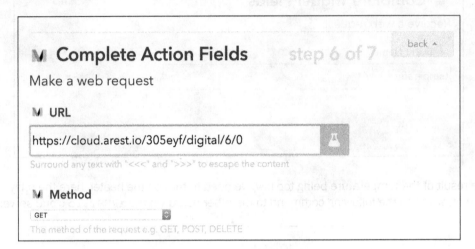

You can now create those two recipes, and observe the project in action. If the temperature gets too low, for example, you should see the relay being activated automatically. You can, of course, connect the project to an actual heater instead of a relay, for example, using the PowerSwitch Tail component.

How it works...

This project works by using IFTTT to make the link between the two boards, therefore building a simple thermostat system in which the components are communicating via the cloud.

 Note that we had to define a margin of 1 degree around the target temperature inside the code. Without this system of two effective thresholds, the system will constantly send alerts once the temperature is around the target temperature.

See also

I now recommend checking the final recipe of this chapter, to learn how to control several home automation projects from a single dashboard.

Home automation dashboard in the cloud

In the last recipe of this chapter, we are going to integrate several projects we saw in this chapter, and see how to monitor them all within a single cloud dashboard. You will then have a complete home automation that can be monitored from anywhere using a single interface.

Getting ready

For this recipe, we are going to use previous projects from this chapter, so I will ask you to refer to the respective recipes of this chapter to build the different projects. We are first going to use a project with a DHT11 sensor, to measure the temperature and humidity in your home. Then, we'll add a smoke sensor into our home automation system.

Finally, we are also going to use the PowerSwitch Tail again to control a lamp remotely:

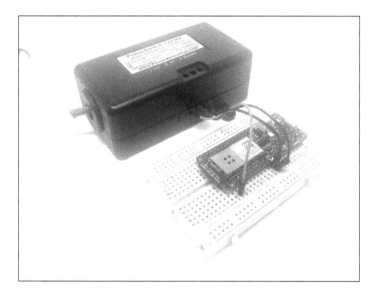

How to do it...

Once all the three projects are assembled, make sure to configure them all with their respective sketches that you will find inside the GitHub repository of this book at `https://github.com/marcoschwartz/iot-arduino-cookbook`.

Of course, make sure to modify each of the sketches with your own Wi-Fi credentials, and also modify the ID of each board. Then, go over to `http://dashboard.arest.io/`.

You can now create a new dashboard:

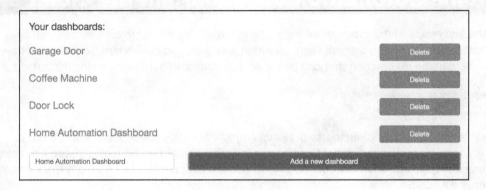

Let's start by adding the reading from the **Gas Sensor**:

Then, you can add a digital **On/Off** control on pin 6 to control the lamp or any device attached to the PowerSwitch Tail:

Finally, add the element for the temperature readout:

You can complete the dashboard by adding an element for the humidity:

Home Automation Dashboard

Gas Sensor		47			gas_sensor	ONLINE
Lamp Control	On	Off	LOW		lamp_control	ONLINE
Temperature		28			sensor	ONLINE
Humidity		31			sensor	ONLINE

Congratulations, you now have all the elements of your basic home automation system in a single cloud dashboard!

How it works...

The project is based on the same aREST framework that we used a lot in this chapter. Here, we saw how to integrate several Arduino boards into the same cloud dashboard.

You can, of course, now add more boards into the same dashboard, to have a larger home automation system that can be monitored and controlled from anywhere.

See also

As this was the last recipe of this chapter, I now recommend checking the next section in case you had any issues when building the projects of this book.

Troubleshooting home automation project issues

In this part of the chapter, we are going to see what can go wrong when building home automation systems in the cloud using the Arduino MKR1000 board. Indeed, some of the steps involved here are quite complex and many things can go differently than expected.

The smoke detector constantly sends alerts

If the smoke detector is constantly sending you alerts but no smoke is present, go back to the calibration stage and adjust the potentiometer to the desired value. Then, make sure that you place a threshold above this value inside the code, so it will only send you alerts when smoke is actually present.

Dashboard

If you correctly configured your boards but can't see them as online inside the dashboard, there are many things you can check. First, check that you changed the ID inside the code, and that you also entered the exact same ID in the dashboard. Also open the Serial monitor and make sure you can see that the board is indeed connected to the cloud server.

6

Fun Internet of Things Projects

In this chapter, we will cover:

- ▶ Making a simple Arduino clock
- ▶ Building a digital candle
- ▶ A cloud-controlled digital candle
- ▶ Building a Bitcoin ticker with Arduino
- ▶ Assembling a GPS module
- ▶ Building a simple GPS tracker
- ▶ Troubleshooting fun IoT project issues

Introduction

In this chapter, we are going to have some fun, and apply all that we saw so far in the book to simple, entertaining, but also useful IoT projects that use Arduino. In these examples, we are going to build a clock that gets the time from the cloud, and also an actual GPS tracker that will display the position of your Arduino project on Google Maps!

Making a simple Arduino clock

As the first project of this chapter, we are going to build a simple clock that gets the time from a cloud server, using Arduino. The time itself will actually be displayed on an OLED screen, also controlled by the Arduino board.

Getting ready

For this project, you will need an OLED screen to display the time that can be controlled via Arduino. I recommend using the 128x64 OLED screen from Adafruit (`https://www.adafruit.com/products/938`).

We can now assemble the project, which basically consists of simply connecting the Arduino board to the OLED screen. First, place both boards on a breadboard. Then, connect the VIN pin of the OLED board to the VCC of the Arduino board, and GND to GND. After that, connect the data and clock pins: data goes to the SDA of the Arduino board, and CLK goes to the SCL of the Arduino board. Finally, connect the RST pin of the OLED screen to pin 4 of the Arduino board.

This is the final result:

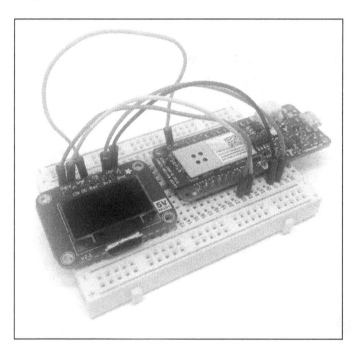

On the software side, you will need to download the Adafruit_SSD1306 library and the RTCZero library. You can easily get them by using the Arduino libraries manager.

How to do it...

Let's now see how to configure the project. As usual, you will find the complete code inside the GitHub repository of the book, as it's too complex and long to be inserted here.

It starts by including the required libraries:

```
#include <SPI.h>
#include <Wire.h>
#include <Adafruit_SSD1306.h>
#include <WiFi101.h>
#include <WiFiUdp.h>
#include <RTCZero.h>
```

Next, you need to define your Wi-Fi network name and password:

```
char ssid[] = "wifi-name";  //  your network SSID (name)
char pass[] = "wifi-pass"; // your network password
```

We also create an instance of the RTC library that we will use to access the real-time clock of the Arduino board:

```
RTCZero rtc;
```

Right after that, we set up the required parameters for the OLED screen:

```
#define OLED_RESET 4
Adafruit_SSD1306 display(OLED_RESET);
#define LOGO16_GLCD_HEIGHT 16
#define LOGO16_GLCD_WIDTH  16

#if (SSD1306_LCDHEIGHT != 64)
#error("Height incorrect, please fix Adafruit_SSD1306.h!');
#endif
```

We also initialize the RTC with some values:

```
rtc.begin();
rtc.setTime(hours, minutes, seconds);
rtc.setDate(day, month, year);
```

Those don't really matter, as we will only display the time and the time will be grabbed from a remote server.

The most important part is displaying the time inside the `loop()` function of the sketch. First, we have to define the size, color, and position of the text:

```
display.setTextSize(2);
display.setTextColor(WHITE);
display.setCursor(16,24);
```

Then, we display the time, using the RTC that was updated from the data from the time server:

```
display.clearDisplay();
  if (rtc.getHours() < 10) {
    display.print('0');
  }
  display.print(rtc.getHours());
  display.print(":");
  if (rtc.getMinutes() < 10) {
    display.print('0');
  }
  display.print(rtc.getMinutes());
  display.print(":");
  if (rtc.getSeconds() < 10) {
    display.print('0');
  }
  display.print(rtc.getSeconds());
  display.display();
```

It's now time to test the sketch! Grab all the code from the GitHub repository of the book, and make sure to modify the Wi-Fi parameters inside the code. Then, upload the code to the board. You should quickly see the time being displayed on the OLED screen:

Congratulations, you have just built a cloud-synchronized clock using Arduino!

How it works...

The project works by grabbing the current time from a time server using the Wi-Fi connectivity of the Arduino MKR1000 board. Then, this time is stored inside the real-time clock of the Arduino board, and is then displayed on the OLED screen.

See also

I now recommend checking more recipes in this chapter to learn how to build more fun and exciting IoT projects!

Building a digital candle

In this recipe, we are going to learn how to make a digital version of a candle using Arduino. We'll see how to control a multicolor LED to emulate the behavior of a real candle. It's just the perfect project for Valentine's Day, Christmas, and other celebrations.

Getting ready

For this project, the only thing you will need is an Adafruit NeoPixel, which is a smart RGB LED that can be easily controlled via Arduino.

I also used some alligator clips to connect the Arduino board to the NeoPixel.

Assembling the project is really easy – you just need to connect the NeoPixel input pin to Arduino pin 5, GND to GND, and VCC to VCC of the Arduino board.

This is the final result:

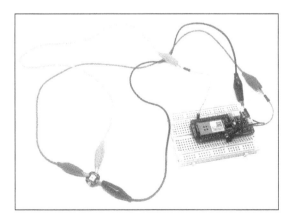

On the software side, the only thing you need is to install the `Adafruit_NeoPixel` library, which you can install from the Arduino library manager.

How to do it...

Let's now see how to configure the project. The first step is to include the required library, and declare that the NeoPixel is connected to pin 5:

```
#include <Adafruit_NeoPixel.h>
#define PIN 5
```

Then, we define three variables that will set the yellowish color of the flame:

```
int redPx = 255;
int grnHigh = 135;
int bluePx = 15;
```

After that, we create an instance of the `NeoPixel`:

```
Adafruit_NeoPixel strip = Adafruit_NeoPixel(1, PIN, NEO_GRB + NEO_
KHZ800);
```

In the `setup()` function, we initialize the `NeoPixel`, and also start it:

```
strip.begin();
strip.show();
```

Inside the `loop()` function, we call a series of functions that will emulate the behavior of the flame:

```
burn(10);
flicker(5);
burn(8);
flutter(6);
burn(3);
on(10);
burn(10);
flicker(10);
```

You can read the description of each of those functions inside the sketch, and actually create your own candle behavior by playing with the order of those functions and also with the timings.

It's finally time to test our digital candle! You can just grab the code from the GitHub repository of the book and upload it to the board. You should immediately see the NeoPixel start to flicker and behave like a flame.

To make it look much better, I actually placed it inside a glass container, with some thin transparent paper around. This gave it a really nice appearance as the light diffused through the paper:

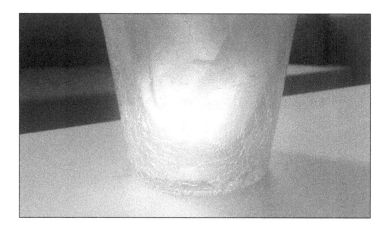

How it works...

This project works by emulating the behavior of an actual flame by using an RGB LED and a set of functions inside the Arduino sketch. By doing so, and by placing our Arduino project inside a glass container along with transparent paper, we can build a completely configurable digital candle.

See also

I now recommend checking the next recipe to learn how to control the candle from the cloud.

A cloud-controlled digital candle

In the previous recipe, we learned how to build a digital candle using Arduino. But what about the IoT aspect of the project? Well, this is what we are going to deal with in this recipe. We are going to connect the project from the previous recipe to the cloud, and learn how to control it from anywhere. This could, for example, be a candle that you send to loved ones that are far away, and that you suddenly switch on to show you are thinking about them.

Getting ready

For this project, first you need to follow the previous recipe to build the candle. Then, you can configure the candle with some new code to control it from the cloud.

You will need to install the `PubSubClient` and `aREST` libraries, which you can easily do by using the Arduino library manager.

The sketch starts as always with the required libraries:

```
#include <SPI.h>
#include <WiFi101.h>
#include <PubSubClient.h>
#include <aREST.h>
#include <Adafruit_NeoPixel.h>
#define PIN 5
```

Then, you can set your Wi-Fi name and password:

```
const char* ssid     = "wifi-name';
const char* password = "wifi-pass';
```

We also set a unique ID for the device:

```
rest.set_id("01e48c');
rest.set_name("candle');
```

We also define a mechanism to turn the candle on and off from the cloud. For that, we'll use a simple variable:

```
if (candleState == true) {
    burn(10);
    flicker(5);
    burn(8);
    flutter(6);
    burn(3);
    on(10);
    burn(10);
    flicker(10);
}
else {
    strip.setPixelColor(0, 1, 1, 1);
    strip.show();
}
```

We also define a function called `candleControl` that will switch the state of the variable that controls the candle:

```
int candleControl(String command) {

    candleState = !candleState;
    return 1;
}
```

You can now grab the code from GitHub, modify it with your own Wi-Fi credentials, and then upload it to the board. You should see that for now, the candle is off. We'll now see how to activate it from the cloud.

How to do it...

We are now going to see how to control the candle from a cloud dashboard. If you haven't done so already, create an account at `http://dashboard.arest.io/`.

You can then create a new dashboard for the candle:

Then, create a new element for the candle, by indicating the ID of your project, and by selecting the `candle` function:

You should then see that your device is online:

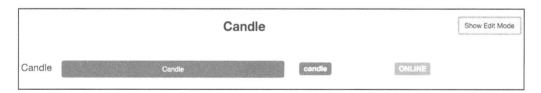

You can now try it. A simple press on the button should almost immediately switch the candle on. Another click will shut it off again. You can now control your digital candle from anywhere in the world!

How it works...

This project makes use of the aREST cloud platform to control the candle remotely, and activate it from a cloud dashboard.

See also

I now recommend checking the rest of this chapter for more fun IoT projects with Arduino!

Building a Bitcoin ticker with Arduino

Bitcoin is currently the most used cryptocurrency in the world. There are a lot of Bitcoin tickers (plugins or websites that indicate the current price of Bitcoin) out there, but wouldn't it be cool if you could have your own little Bitcoin ticker on your desk? This is exactly what we are going to do in this recipe.

Getting ready

For the hardware, you can refer to the very first recipe of this chapter, as it uses exactly the same hardware that we use in this project: an OLED screen connected to the Arduino MKR1000 board.

Let's now see how to configure the project. As the sketch is quite long, I will only highlight the most important parts here. First, we define the Wi-Fi credentials, and we also define the API that we'll use to grab the current price of Bitcoin:

```
// WiFi settings
const char* ssid     = "Jarex_5A';
const char* password = "connect1337';

// API server
const char* host = "api.coindesk.com';
```

Then, in the `loop()` function of the sketch, we create a Wi-Fi client and connect to the API server:

```
WiFiClient client;
  const int httpPort = 80;
  if (!client.connect(host, httpPort)) {
    Serial.println("connection failed');
    return;
  }
```

hen, we create the request to get the current price of Bitcoin, and send it to the server:

```
// We now create a URI for the request
String url = "/v1/bpi/currentprice.json';

Serial.print("Requesting URL: ");
Serial.println(url);

// This will send the request to the server
client.print(String("GET ") + url + " HTTP/1.1\r\n' +
             "Host: " + host + "\r\n' +
             "Connection: close\r\n\r\n');
delay(100);
```

After that, we read the answer from the server:

```
String answer;
while(client.available()){
  String line = client.readStringUntil('\r');
  answer += line;
}
```

After a lot of formatting of the answer that I won't detail here, we print the price of Bitcoin on the OLED screen:

```
// Print price
Serial.println();
Serial.println("Bitcoin price: ");
Serial.println(price);

// Display on OLED
display.setTextSize(3);
display.setTextColor(WHITE);
display.setCursor(10,24);

display.clearDisplay();
display.print(priceString);
display.display();
```

How to do it...

You can now grab the code from the GitHub repository of the book, modify it with your own Wi-Fi credentials, and then upload the code to the board. You should then quickly see the current price of Bitcoin appearing on your OLED screen:

How it works...

The project uses the Wi-Fi connection of the Arduino MKR1000 board to connect to a server that serves the Bitcoin price via an API, and then displays this price on the OLED screen.

See also

I recommend checking the next two recipes to build another cool project: making a GPS module with Arduino.

Assembling a GPS module

In this recipe, we are going to learn how to completely assemble a GPS module with Arduino, and make sure that it is working. The goal is to build a GPS tracking module with Arduino, which is what we will see in the next recipe.

Getting ready

For this project, we will have to use an Arduino Uno board, instead of the usual MKR1000 board, as at the time of writing, the GPS/GSM module I used was not compatible with the MKR1000 board. This is the list of all the components that you will need for this recipe:

- Arduino Uno (https://www.sparkfun.com/products/11021)
- Adafruit Fona 808 breakout (http://www.adafruit.com/product/2542)
- GSM uFL antenna (http://www.adafruit.com/products/1991)
- GSM SIM card with GPRS data available
- 3.7V LiPo battery (http://www.adafruit.com/products/328)
- LiPo battery charger (http://www.adafruit.com/products/1904)
- Passive GPS antenna (https://www.adafruit.com/product/2461)
- Breadboard (https://www.sparkfun.com/products/12002)
- Jumper wires (https://www.sparkfun.com/products/8431)

Let's now assemble all those components. First, insert the SIM card inside the slot on the GSM/GPS shield:

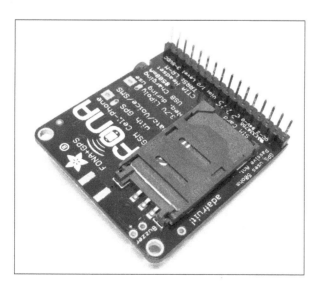

Next, you need to make the following connections between the Arduino board and the GSM/GPS module:

- ▸ Vio connects to 5V of the Arduino board
- ▸ GND connects to GND
- ▸ Key connects to GND as well
- ▸ RX connects to digital 2 of the Arduino board
- ▸ TX connects to digital 3 of the Arduino board
- ▸ RST connects to digital pin 4 of the Arduino board

Also connect the GPS and GSM antennas to the module. This is the final result:

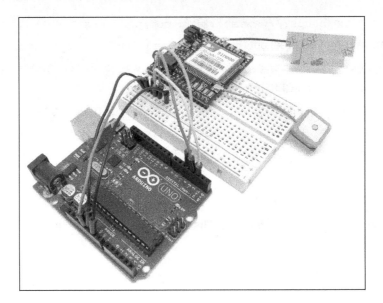

Just before using the project, also connect the battery to the GSM/GPS module via the JST connector.

You will also need the Adafruit_FONA library, which you can get using the Arduino library manager.

How to do it...

Let's now quickly test this project to see if it works correctly. First, we need to import the required libraries:

```
#include "Adafruit_FONA.h'
#include <SoftwareSerial.h>
```

Then, we create the different instances required for the GPS module:

```
// Instances
SoftwareSerial fonaSS = SoftwareSerial(FONA_TX, FONA_RX);
SoftwareSerial *fonaSerial = &fonaSS;

// Fona instance
Adafruit_FONA fona = Adafruit_FONA(FONA_RST);
```

Inside the `loop()` function of the sketch, we query the data from the GPS module:

```
char gpsdata[120];
  fona.getGPS(0, gpsdata, 120);
  if (type == FONA808_V1)
    Serial.println(F("Reply in format: mode,longitude,latitude,altitud
e,utctime(yyyymmddHHMMSS),ttff,satellites,speed,course'));
  else
    Serial.println(F("Reply in format: mode,fixstatus,utctime(yyyymmd
dHHMMSS),latitude,longitude,altitude,speed,course,fixmode,reserved1,
HDOP,PDOP,VDOP,reserved2,view_satellites,used_satellites,reserved3,C/
N0max,HPA,VPA'));
  Serial.println(gpsdata);
```

We then convert this data to numeric coordinates, which can be used to locate the project on Google Maps, and we print this information on the `Serial` port:

```
String latitude = getLatitudeGPS(gpsdata);
  String longitude = getLongitudeGPS(gpsdata);

  float latitudeNumeric = convertDegMinToDecDeg(latitude.toFloat());
  float longitudeNumeric = convertDegMinToDecDeg(longitude.toFloat());

  Serial.print("Latitude, longitude: ");
  Serial.print(latitudeNumeric, 4);
  Serial.print(",');
  Serial.println(longitudeNumeric, 4);
```

Finally, grab the code from the GitHub repository of the book, and upload it to the board. Also make sure that the battery is connected to the module, and that you also place the GPS antenna in a place with a direct line of sight with the sky (it usually won't work indoors unless you are close to a window).

Then, open the Serial monitor. You should see the following output:

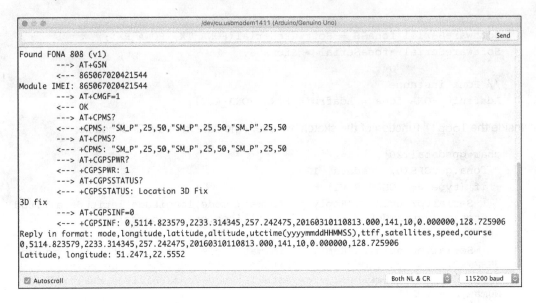

```
/dev/cu.usbmodem1411 (Arduino/Genuino Uno)
                                                                    Send
Found FONA 808 (v1)
        ---> AT+GSN
        <--- 865067020421544
Module IMEI: 865067020421544
        ---> AT+CMGF=1
        <--- OK
        ---> AT+CPMS?
        <--- +CPMS: "SM_P",25,50,"SM_P",25,50,"SM_P",25,50
        ---> AT+CPMS?
        <--- +CPMS: "SM_P",25,50,"SM_P",25,50,"SM_P",25,50
        ---> AT+CGPSPWR?
        <--- +CGPSPWR: 1
        ---> AT+CGPSSTATUS?
        <--- +CGPSSTATUS: Location 3D Fix
3D fix
        ---> AT+CGPSINF=0
        <--- +CGPSINF: 0,5114.823579,2233.314345,257.242475,20160310110813.000,141,10,0.000000,128.725906
Reply in format: mode,longitude,latitude,altitude,utctime(yyyymmddHHMMSS),ttff,satellites,speed,course
0,5114.823579,2233.314345,257.242475,20160310110813.000,141,10,0.000000,128.725906
Latitude, longitude: 51.2471,22.5552

☑ Autoscroll                                    Both NL & CR  ◇   115200 baud ◇
```

You can now actually copy the result, and paste it into Google Maps: you should immediately see your own current location on the map!

How it works...

This project works by using the GPS module to find the current location of the project, and printing it on the Serial monitor. This test was simply to make sure that the GPS was working correctly, before building a GPS tracker.

See also

I now really recommend checking the next recipe to transform this project into a GPS tracker.

Building a simple GPS tracker

In the last recipe of this chapter, we are going to build a simple GPS tracker using the hardware we built in the previous recipe. We will send the current GPS location of the project to a cloud server, and then use this to display the position of the project in real time on a Google Maps widget.

Getting ready

You will, of course, need to have built the hardware in the previous recipe, and make sure that the GPS is working correctly. If that's not done yet, please refer to the previous recipe.

Let's now see how to configure the project so that it sends data to **Dweet.io**, which is a cloud server we already used in this book. As the code is quite long, I will only highlight the most important parts here.

First, let's define a new thing called `gps_tracker`:

```
String dweetThing = "gps_tracker';
```

Inside the `loop()` function of the sketch, we create a new request to Dweet.io, by including the latitude, longitude, and battery level inside the request:

```
uint16_t statuscode;
  int16_t length;
  char url[80];
  String request = "www.dweet.io/dweet/for/';
  request += dweetThing;
  request += "?latitude=' + String(latitudeNumeric);
  request += "&longitude=' + String(longitudeNumeric);
  request += "&battery=' + String(vbat);
  request.toCharArray(url, request.length());
```

We then send this request to Dweet.io using the GPRS data connection of the module:

```
if (!fona.HTTP_GET_start(url, &statuscode, (uint16_t *)&length)) {
    Serial.println("Failed!');
  }
  while (length > 0) {
    while (fona.available()) {
      char c = fona.read();

      // Serial.write is too slow, we'll write directly to Serial
  register!
```

```
    #if defined(__AVR_ATmega328P__) || defined(__AVR_ATmega168__)
        loop_until_bit_is_set(UCSR0A, UDRE0); /* Wait until data
register empty. */
        UDR0 = c;
    #else
        Serial.write(c);
    #endif
        length--;
    }
  }
  fona.HTTP_GET_end();
```

How to do it...

You can, of course, grab the complete code for this project on the GitHub repository of the book. Then, upload the code to the board, making sure to enter your own setting for your GPRS data provider inside the sketch (username and password if you need one).

Then, open the Serial monitor. You should see a similar message to the following:

```
Status: 200
Len: 217
        ---> AT+HTTPREAD
        <--- +HTTPREAD: 2t7
is":"succeeded","by":"dweeting","the":"dweet","with":{"thing":"gps_tracker","created":"2016-(
        <--- OK
Waiting until next message...
        ---> AT+CGPSINF=0
```

| Autoscroll | Both NL & CR | 115200 baud |

If you can see that, it means that the data has been successfully transmitted to Dweet.io, and stored on the cloud.

Then, we are going to set a dashboard so you can follow the location of the tracker on Google Maps. If you haven't done so yet, create an account at `http://freeboard.io/`.

There, create a new dashboard, and a new data source inside this dashboard with the following parameters:

Then, add a new pane, and create a new Google Map widget inside the pane, linking it to the data source you created before:

You should immediately see your own location on the map:

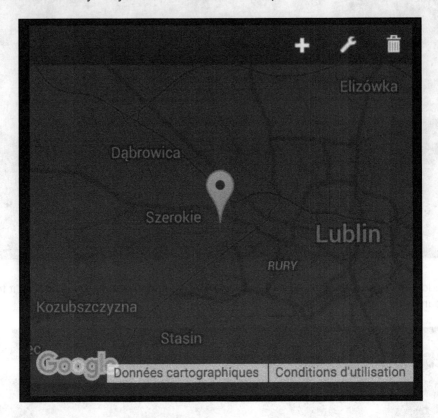

Of course, this location is refreshed regularly, making it a real GPS tracker using Arduino!

How it works...

This project works by using all the functionalities of the GSM/GPS shield: it uses the GPRS connection of the shield to send the location that is acquired via the GPS module in real time. Then, we used a cloud dashboard to display the location of the project on a map.

See also

As this was the last recipe in this chapter, I now recommend checking the next section in case you had issues with the recipes in this chapter.

Troubleshooting fun IoT project issues

In this part of the chapter, we are going to see what can go wrong when configuring your board and connecting it to the Internet. Indeed, some of the steps involved here are quite complex and many things can go differently than expected.

Nothing is displayed on the OLED screen

The first thing that can happen is that the OLED module has not been correctly connected to the Arduino board. For example, you could have mixed the SCL and SDA pins. Also make sure that you have correctly connected the reset pin. Then, make sure that the Wi-Fi credentials have been correctly entered in the sketch.

I can't get my location using the GPS module

The GPS module that I used in this chapter really needs to have a clear line of sight with the sky to work correctly, unlike the more advanced modules that you have in your phone, for example. So if the project doesn't work, make sure the module is close to a window or even slightly outside. Also make sure that you have connected a fully-charged battery to the project.

7
Mobile Robot Applications

In this chapter, we will cover:

- ▶ Choosing a robotic platform
- ▶ Building a mobile robot
- ▶ Configuring your mobile robot
- ▶ Basic robot control
- ▶ Using distance sensors
- ▶ Controlling your robot from anywhere
- ▶ Troubleshooting basic robotic issues

Introduction

Building mobile robots is one of the most entertaining things you can do with the Arduino platform. Because the platform is so easy to use, you will be able to create mobile robots in no time, and also control them from the Internet.

In this last chapter of the book, we are going to see how to create your own mobile robot based on Arduino. We'll see how to choose a nice robotic platform, and how to assemble your first mobile robot. Then, we are going to see how to control this robot locally from your web browser, and we'll also mount an ultrasonic distance sensor on the robot so it can detect obstacles. Finally, to end this book about the Internet of Things, we are going to learn how to control this robot from anywhere in the world.

Choosing a robotic platform

The first step that you need to take in order to build a nice mobile robot is to choose the correct platform. There are many choices available that are compatible with the Arduino MKR1000 board. We are going to review these options, and also choose a platform for the rest of the chapter.

Choosing a platform

The first kind of robots that are available are two-wheeled robots, such as this chassis from Emgreat:

These platforms usually come with two motors already mounted on the robot, along with two wheels and a flywheel in front of the robot. They are easy to use, and you can usually mount an Arduino board on them.

You also have four-wheeled robots, such as this other product from Emgreat:

These are more stable than the two-wheeled platforms, but they are also more complex to control as you need to control four independent DC motors in the code of the Arduino board.

Finally, you have Rover platforms, which are basically like the four-wheeled robots, but with continuous tracks instead of wheels:

The advantage of these platforms is that you can actually control them with only two motors, while keeping a good stability of the platform because of the continuous tracks. This is the kind of platform that I will be using for the rest of this chapter.

There's more...

There are, of course, several other platforms out there that would be just as compatible with Arduino so I invite you to look on the Web to find the platform that's best suited for your projects!

See also

I now recommend checking the next recipe to learn how to build your mobile robot!

Building a mobile robot

In this recipe, we are going to see which components we need to build a mobile robot based on Arduino, and of course how to build the robot itself. At the end of the recipe, you will have a fully-functional mobile robot that is ready to be programmed.

Getting ready

As we saw in the previous recipe, we are going to use a rover-like robot platform for this chapter. The one I selected comes with the chassis, but also with two DC motors already built-in. Of course, you can use the platform of your choice, but you will need to adapt the different recipes of this book for any other platform.

This is the list of components that you will need for the whole chapter, excluding the Arduino MKR1000 board:

- ► Rover robot chassis with two motors (http://www.dfrobot.com/index.php?route=product/product&product_id=390)
- ► L293D motor driver (https://www.adafruit.com/products/807)
- ► 4xAA battery pack (https://www.sparkfun.com/products/9835)
- ► 3.7V LiPo battery (https://www.sparkfun.com/products/8483)
- ► URM37 ultrasonic sensor (http://www.tinyosshop.com/index.php?route=product/product&product_id=104)
- ► Breadboard (https://www.sparkfun.com/products/12002)
- ► Jumper wires (https://www.sparkfun.com/products/9194)

On the software side, you will need the aREST and PubSub libraries for Arduino that we already installed in previous chapters.

How to do it...

Let's now see how to assemble the robot, and integrate the Arduino MKR1000 board on it. First, we are going to connect the Arduino MKR1000 board to the motors and to the battery pack. As the process is a bit complicated, I created a schematic that you can simply follow to make the correct connections:

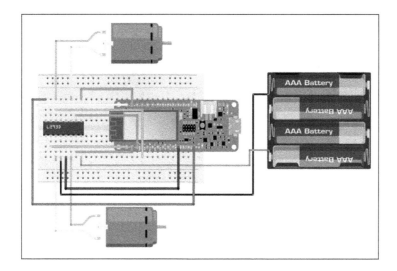

This is the final result, not showing the motors and the battery pack:

This is a view of the mobile robot platform, just after I bought it:

This is the battery pack that I will be using for this project, along with four 1.2V rechargeable batteries:

Finally, just put everything inside the robot chassis, you can always make things prettier after testing the robot.

This is the final result:

How it works...

In this recipe, we assembled all the components to make a basic mobile robot around the Arduino MKR1000 board. The Arduino board will be able to control the robot using the L293D motor driver, which is a chip dedicated to controlling DC motors.

See also

Now that we have a fully assembled mobile robot, I recommend checking the next recipe to learn how to configure it and make sure it works correctly.

Configuring your mobile robot

In this recipe, we are simply going to make sure that the robot we assembled is working correctly, by testing the motors of the robot. This will allow us to be sure that everything is working later when it comes to writing more complex sketches to control the robot.

Getting ready

Here, you simply need to make sure that you followed the previous recipe to assemble the robot. Also make sure that the batteries are fully charged, and that the robot's wheels or tracks are not touching the ground, as we simply want to test the motors here.

How to do it...

We are now going to build a sketch to test the motors of the robot. As a test, we'll make the robot go forward, and then stop, and repeat the process.

First, we define which pins the L293D chip is connected to on the Arduino board:

```
// Define motor pins
int motorOnePlus = 6;
int motorOneMinus = 7;
int motorOneEnable = 5;

int motorTwoPlus = 8;
int motorTwoMinus = 9;
int motorTwoEnable = 4;
```

After that, in the `setup()` function of the sketch, we set all those pins as outputs:

```
Serial.begin(1152000);

// Set pins
pinMode(motorOnePlus, OUTPUT);
pinMode(motorOneMinus, OUTPUT);
pinMode(motorOneEnable, OUTPUT);

pinMode(motorTwoPlus, OUTPUT);
pinMode(motorTwoMinus, OUTPUT);
pinMode(motorTwoEnable, OUTPUT);

}
```

Then, in the `loop()` function of the sketch, we first make both motors rotate in one direction at about half the maximum speed, and then we stop them again:

```
// Accelerate forward
setMotorOne(true, 500);
setMotorTwo(true, 500);

// Delay
delay(5000);
// Stop
setMotorOne(true, 0);
setMotorTwo(true, 0);

// Delay
delay(5000);
```

Let's now have a look at the functions that we use to control the motors:

```
// Function to control the motor
void setMotorOne(boolean forward, int motor_speed){
    digitalWrite(motorOnePlus, forward);
    digitalWrite(motorOneMinus, !forward);
    analogWrite(motorOneEnable, motor_speed);
}
// Function to control the motor
void setMotorTwo(boolean forward, int motor_speed){
    digitalWrite(motorTwoPlus, forward);
    digitalWrite(motorTwoMinus, !forward);
    analogWrite(motorTwoEnable, motor_speed);
}
```

Basically, we always need to apply opposite signals on the direction pins, and then we use an `analogWrite()` function to set the speed of the motors.

You can now upload the sketch to the Arduino board. You should see that the robot is first accelerating forward, and then stopping. If this is happening, congratulations, you can control a mobile robot using the Arduino MKR1000 board!

How it works...

This sketch is using the L293D circuit connected to the Arduino board to control the robot. We have basically created functions that allow us to control the motors from the Arduino boards, and we'll be using the same functions in the upcoming recipes of this chapter.

See also

You can now move on to the next recipe to learn how to actually make the robot move around.

Basic robot control

In this recipe, we are finally going to dive into the core of this chapter: making our robot move around! We'll learn how to configure it so it can receive commands via Wi-Fi, and then we'll learn how to control it using a simple interface running inside your browser.

Getting ready

For this recipe, just make sure that you followed all the recipes so far in the chapter. Also, it is recommended to leave the robot in a position where the wheels or track are not touching the ground, at least till you are sure it is working correctly.

How to do it...

We are now going to program the robot so it accepts commands via Wi-Fi. For that, we'll use the aREST framework that we have already used several times in this book.

The sketch starts by including the required libraries:

```
#include <SPI.h>
#include <WiFi101.h>
#include <aREST.h>
```

Then, you need to define your Wi-Fi network name and password:

```
char ssid[] = "wifi-name';
char password[] = "wifi-pass';
```

After that, we declare several functions that we will use to control the robot:

```
int stop(String command);
int forward(String command);
int left(String command);
int right(String command);
int backward(String command);
```

Inside the `setup()` function of the sketch, we expose these functions to the aREST API:

```
rest.function("forward', forward);
rest.function("stop', stop);
rest.function("right', right);
rest.function("left', left);
rest.function("backward', backward);
```

In the `loop()` function, we listen for incoming connections, and process them using aREST:

```
// Handle REST calls
  WiFiClient client = server.available();
  if (!client) {
    return;
  }
  while(!client.available()){
    delay(1);
  }
  rest.handle(client);
```

Let's now have a look at one of those functions to control the robot:

```
int forward(String command) {

  setMotorOne(true, 1000);
  setMotorTwo(true, 1000);

}
```

As we can see, it uses the functions we used in the previous recipe to test the robot. For example, the forward function makes both motors go in the same direction at nearly maximum speed.

You can now grab the code from the GitHub repository of the book, and configure the Arduino board with it. Don't forget to modify the Wi-Fi credentials in the sketch. For now, just open the Serial monitor after uploading the code to get the IP address of the board, we'll need it in a moment.

We are now going to create an interface to control the robot via push buttons. I'll only describe the main parts of the code here, but you can find all the code from the GitHub repository of the book.

The code is based on one HTML file (for the interface) and one JavaScript file (for sending the commands to the robot).

Inside the HTML file, we define several buttons to control the robot, for example, to make it move forward:

```
<div class='row'>

  <div class='col-md-5'></div>
  <div class='col-md-2'>
    <button id='forward' class='btn btn-primary btn-block'
type='button'>Forward</button>
  </div>
  <div class='col-md-5'></div>

</div>
```

The JavaScript file is making use of aREST.js, a very convenient library made to control aREST projects via JavaScript. You can find out more about it at https://github.com/marcoschwartz/aREST.js.

Inside the JavaScript file, we need to set the IP of the board:

```
var address = "192.168.0.104';
var device = new Device(address);
```

Then, we link each of the buttons to an action, for example, the **forward** button:

```
$('#forward').mousedown(function() {
  device.callFunction("forward');
});
$('#forward').mouseup(function() {
  device.callFunction("stop');
});
```

Note that in order to obtain a push-button behavior, we always call the `stop()` function on the robot whenever a button is released.

You can now simply get the interface files from the GitHub repository of the book, and modify the IP address in the code. Then, open the HTML file with your favorite web browser:

You can now try it: just press the forward button, for example, and the robot should go forward. Whenever you release the button, the robot should immediately stop. You can, of course, play with the other buttons to control the robot.

At this point, the robot should still be linked to your computer via USB. To solve this issue, simply power the Arduino board using the 3.7V LiPo battery, and get a completely wireless mobile robot!

How it works...

This whole recipe is based on the aREST library, which we used to send commands to the robot via Wi-Fi. Using a simple web interface, we can then easily control the robot from a web browser.

In the next recipe in the chapter, we are going to add a distance sensor to the robot to know if there is any obstacle in front of it.

Using distance sensors

For now, we are able to control our mobile robot, but except if we directly look at it, we have no way of knowing if there is an obstacle in front of it.

This is where ultrasonic sensors come into play: they are an easy, inexpensive way to know precisely if there is something in front of the mobile robot, and at what distance. In this recipe, we'll add an ultrasonic sensor to our robot and integrate it into the interface.

Getting ready

The first thing you need is, of course, an ultrasonic sensor. For this project, I used an URM37 ultrasonic sensor from DFRobot:

This is the back of the sensor, showing all the pins:

You can now mount the sensor on the robot's chassis, putting the sensor in front of the robot.

Then, you can refer to the documentation at `http://www.dfrobot.com/wiki/index. php?title=URM37_V4.0_Ultrasonic_Sensor_(SKU:SEN0001)` to find the pins of the sensor.

Basically, you need to connect the VCC pin to the VCC pin of the Arduino board, GND to GND, and pin number 4 of the sensor (ECHO) to Arduino pin A0.

This is the final result:

How to do it...

Let's now see how to integrate the sensor into the code. First, we expose a function called
measureDistance to the aREST API:

```
rest.function("distance', measureDistance);
```

This is the details of this function that returns the distance in front of the robot in centimeters:

```
int measureDistance(String command) {

  // Measure distance
  unsigned int Distance = 0;
  unsigned long DistanceMeasured = pulseIn(distanceSensorPin, LOW);

  // Compute distance
  if (DistanceMeasured == 50000 ) {
    Serial.print("Invalid');
  }
```

```
    else {
       Distance = DistanceMeasured/50;
    }

    return Distance;

}
```

We also modify the code of the interface to integrate this information, and we perform a measurement on the robot two times every second. You can check the updated code of the interface from the GitHub repository of the book.

Now, upload the new code to the robot, and then open the modified interface. Make sure that you have the correct IP address set in the code.

This is what you should see:

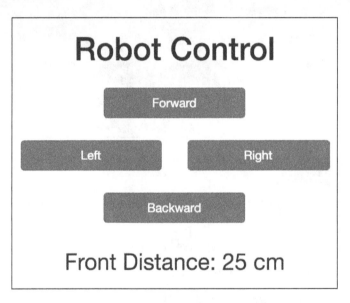

You can still control the robot, but you now also have the distance in front of the robot displayed in the same interface!

How it works...

This project uses an ultrasonic sensor to know the distance in front of the robot. The interface basically calls the function to measure the distance every 500ms, so the information displayed is always up to date as the robot moves around.

There is more...

You can now use this measurement from the ultrasonic sensor in the code, for example, to also make the robot automatically stop when something is detected in front of it.

See also

I now recommend checking the final recipe of the chapter, in which we'll learn how to control the robot from anywhere!

Controlling your robot from anywhere

To end this chapter and this book, we are going to integrate our mobile robot into the Internet of Things, and learn how to control it from anywhere in the world. We'll learn how to call the function we defined earlier from anywhere in the world, and then how to control the robot using a cloud dashboard.

Getting ready

For this final recipe, you just need to have followed all the previous recipes in the chapter.

How to do it...

As the code for this recipe is really similar to the code from previous recipes, I will only highlight the main differences here. You can, of course, refer to the GitHub repository of the book for more details.

You need to include the following libraries:

```
#include <SPI.h>
#include <WiFi101.h>
#include <PubSubClient.h>
#include <aREST.h>
```

Then, an important point here is to define a unique ID for the robot:

```
char* device_id = "40ep12';
```

This will basically identify your robot on the aREST cloud. Then, inside the `loop()` function of the sketch, we simply handle incoming requests with the following:

```
rest.handle(client);
```

You can now grab the code from the GitHub repository of the book, and make sure to modify the Wi-Fi credentials and device ID inside the code. Then, configure the board with this code.

You can now actually test the robot, for example, by calling the `forward` function with the following:

← → C 🔒 https://cloud.arest.io/40ep12/forward

{"return_value": 232, "id": "40ep12", "name": "robot", "connected": true}

Of course, you need to put the correct device ID inside this URL.

Now, we are going to create a simple dashboard to call the essential functions of the robot. For that, refer to `http://dashboard.arest.io/`.

Create an account if you haven't already, and then create a new dashboard:

MRK1000 Robot | Add a new dashboard

Inside this newly created dashboard, create a new element to control the forward function:

| Forward | 40ep12 | Function | forward | Call | Create new element |

Then, repeat the same operation for all the functions of the robot that you want to control:

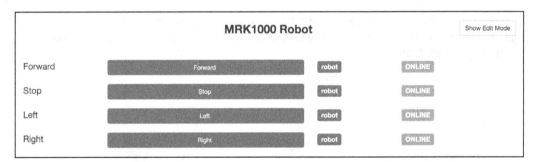

You can now try to control the robot via this cloud dashboard: the robot should answer immediately. You can now control your mobile robot from anywhere in the world!

How it works...

This whole project is based on the aREST framework, which we use here to control our robot using the aREST cloud. Combined with a cloud dashboard, this allows us to control our mobile robot from anywhere in the world.

See also

As this was the last recipe in the chapter, I now recommend checking the next section in case you had trouble in this chapter.

Troubleshooting basic robotic issues

In this part of the chapter, we are going to see what can go wrong when building a mobile robot based on Arduino and controlling it remotely. Indeed, some of the steps involved here are quite complex and many things can go differently than expected.

The motors of the robot don't react to any command

The first thing that can happen is that the motors, or the L293D motor driver haven't been connected correctly to the Arduino board. Make sure that everything is connected correctly according to the schematics found in the relevant recipe. Also make sure that the batteries are fully loaded, or the motors might not have enough power to work correctly.

The interface doesn't work

First make sure that the robot is responding to direct commands via Wi-Fi. For that, you can simply type the IP address of the robot in any browser, followed by the name of the command you want to execute. Also make sure you entered the correct IP address inside the interface JavaScript file.

The ultrasonic sensor returns incorrect readings

First, make sure that the sensor is correctly wired to the Arduino board. Indeed, there are many pins on the URM37 sensor that we used for this task, and it can be easy to make a mistake. Also make sure that the sensor is correctly mounted on the robot chassis, and that it is really measuring distance straight in front of the robot.

The robot can't be accessed from the cloud dashboard

If you can't access the robot from the cloud dashboard, first make sure that you can access it via a web browser, as we saw in the relevant recipe. Then, make sure you entered the correct device ID inside the dashboard.

Index

www.ingramcontent.com/pod-product-compliance
Lightning Source LLC
Chambersburg PA
CBHW060132060326
40690CB00018B/3851